CATHAY

translations & transformations

Heinz Insu Fenkl

Codhill Press

New Paltz ≈ New York

2007

Codhill Press
One Arden Lane
New Paltz, New York 12561
www.codhill.com

Cover illustration by:
John Einarsen,
founding editor and art director, *Kyoto Journal.*
www.kyotojournal.org

Book design by Heinz Insu Fenkl.

"How Master Madman Came to Ch'ing Feng Temple"
originally appeared in The Endicott Studio *Journal of Mythic Arts,* Winter
2006; "Song Bird" originally appeared in *EnterText,*
vol. 3, no. 2, Autumn 2003.

ISBN 1-930337-25-6

For Carolyn —

I hope you have
time to enjoy some of
these translations
and "forgeries"
as you finish
your historical
mystery.

With all my best
from Poughkeepsie,

CATHAY

translations & transformations

'08

For my mentors:

Ben Wallacker
in this world

&

Marian Ury
in the next

The Chinese logograph on the cover of
Ezra Pound's *Cathay* (London: Elkin Matthews, 1915).

Ernest Fenollosa, in his essay, "The Chinese Written Character as a Medium for Poetry" (edited and annotated by Pound), glosses this graph as "rays"—specifically those coming from the moon—but he does not deconstruct its parts the way Pound probably did. It is made of three separate graphs:

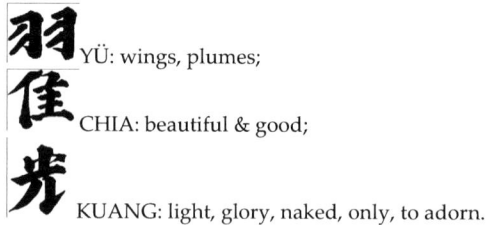

 YÜ: wings, plumes;

 CHIA: beautiful & good;

 KUANG: light, glory, naked, only, to adorn.

I have used the three component graphs as logos throughout this volume to designate epigraphs taken from Pound's *Cathay*. Text that appears under these logographs throughout this volume are translations by Pound. All other translations are my own.

CONTENTS

光

And I let down the crystal curtain
And watch the moon through the clear autumn

—Li Po (701-762)
"The Jewel Stair's Grievance"

Dreaming of Li Po

Death severs us and the sorrow ends,
But with the living gone, I shall grieve forever.
From Chiang-nan, the pestilent land,
Still no news of the banished man.

You entered my dreams, old friend,
Making it clear that I've longed for you,
But now that you are captured,
How have you grown those feathery wings?

I fear it is not your living soul I see—
The way is so immeasurably far,
Your ghost came through the green maple woods
And returned over the dark mountain pass.

The sinking moon fills the roof beams,
And yet I doubt it shines upon your face.
The water is dark, the waves are wide—
Beware the dragons of the deep.

—Tu Fu (712-770)

石橋奇緣

The Fairies on the Bridge

Frontpiece from the 1922 Westminster Press edition;
Kim Man-jung's *A Cloud Dream of the Nine,*
translated by James Scarth Gale.

2

The Reincarnation of Hsing-chen

(from *Nine Cloud Dream* c. 1689)

Kim Man-jung
(1637-1692)

There are five mythic mountains in the East. Near the Yellow Sea lies T'ai-shan, Great Mountain; to west is Hua-shan, Mountain of Flowers; to the south lies Heng-shan, the Mountain of Scales; to the north another Heng-shan, Eternal Mountain; and finally, in the center, stands Sung-shan, the Exalted Mountain. The highest of the five mountains is Heng-shan, south of Tung-t'ing Lake, encircled by the River Hsiang in the other three directions, standing so tall the other mountains look up to it, as if in admiration. In all there are seventy-two peaks upon Heng-shan that rise up and pierce the sky, some jagged and precipitous, blocking the paths of clouds, their fantastic shapes evoking wonder and awe, their auspicious shadows full of good fortune.

Among the seventy-two peaks, the five tallest are called Spirit of the South, Crimson Canopy, Heaven's Pillar, Stone Treasury, and Lotus Peak. They are regal and august, capped by the heavens, with clouds veiling their faces and their bases obscured in mist. They are imbued with divine power, and in the haze of the day they are occluded from human view.

In ancient times, when Yǔ restrained the Great Flood that inundated the earth, he erected a commemorative stone tablet on

3

one of these peaks, recording his many great deeds. The tablet was divinely inscribed in cloud calligraphy, and though many eons have passed, the characters are still sharp and clear.

In the days of Chin Shi Wang Ti, a deva called Queen Wei, having become a Taoist immortal by divine decree, arrived with an attending company of fairies and settled in these mountains. She was known as Queen Wei of the Southern Peak, and many are the strange and wonderful things that she caused to happen there.

In the days of the T'ang Dynasty a great monk arrived from India. He was so taken by the beauty of the mountains that he built a monastery on Lotus Peak, and there he preached the Buddhist sutras, instructed disciples, and banished demons and evil spirits. In time the name of the Gautama Buddha became widely known through him, and people came to pay homage and worship, saying that he himself was a living Buddha who had descended to earth. Those who were rich and noble shared of their material wealth, the poor contributed their labor, and thus a broad and spacious temple came to be built. It was secluded and quiet, with a thousand and one vistas all around—a majestic backdrop of mountains in the distance, a view without equal.

The monk had brought with him a volume of the *Diamond Sutra*, and he explicated it so clearly that they called him "Master of the Six Temptations," the Great Master Liu-kuan. Among the five or six hundred disciples that followed him, there were some thirty who were advanced and well-versed in the teaching, and the youngest of these was Hsing-chen, whose name means "Without Guile." His features were fair and handsome, and a light shone from his face like flowing water. He had already mastered the Three Sacred Books of the *Tripitaka*, though he was barely twenty. He surpassed all the others in wisdom and mental agility, and all knew that the Master loved him best and intended, in time, to make him his successor.

When Master Liu-kuan expounded upon the Dharma to his disciples, the Dragon King himself—in the guise of a white-clad old man—would come from Tung-t'ing Lake to listen and learn. One day the Master called his disciples together and said to them,

"I am old now, and my body is frail. It is has been more than thirteen years since I have been beyond the gates of these mountains. I must go and pay my respects to the Dragon King. Who among you will go in my stead to the Underwater Palace?" Hsing-chen volunteered at once, and the Master was greatly pleased. He had the young monk fitted out in new robes; he presented him with his ringed staff of the gods and speedily sent him off in the direction of Tung-t'ing Lake.

It was just at that moment that the monk who guarded the monastery's main gate came to announce that Queen Wei of the Southern Peak had sent eight fairy messengers to see Master Liu-kuan. They were now waiting outside the gate. The Master commanded that they be admitted and, all modestly in line, they skipped through the gate, circled three times, and bowed, scattering fairy blossoms at his feet. Kneeling respectfully, they recited the message from Queen Wei: "The noble Master lives on the west side of the mountain, I on the east. The distance is not far, and we are near enough to be neighbors. Yet I am of humble birth and am so busy that I have not once visited your sacred temple to hear the Dharma. Lacking wisdom, I know not how best to maintain virtue and propriety, but now I am sending my servants to pay my respects and to offer Your Holiness flowers of paradise, fairy fruit, silks, and other humble gifts. It is my sincerest hope that you will accept them as a token of my earnest heart."

With that, each of the eight fairies presented her flowers and gifts to the Master, and he received them and passed them on to his disciples who, in turn, placed them as offerings before the Buddha. The Master bowed ceremoniously, with hands folded according to custom, and saying, "An old man like me hardly deserves such lavish gifts as these you have presented to me," he gave generously to the fairies in return before they took their leave and set lightly off.

They made their way out through the mountain pass, walking hand in hand and chatting as they went. "The magical mountains of the south are all part of the same range, and they are encircled by the same rivers. In the past, we were at liberty to go anywhere among them. But now that the Great Master Liu-kuan has established his temple, some of the peaks are forbidden to us, and we miss seeing the places of beauty that were once ours to view. We are lucky that our Lady's order brings us to this valley at a beautiful time of year. It is still early, so let us take this chance to climb up to the top and breathe the sweet air of Lotus Peak. Let us dip our scarves in the pure waters, sing a song or two, and rekindle in our souls our joy for life. When we return, we will be admired and envied by our sisters. Let us go!"

They set off, walking skillfully along the high precipices, following the cascading streams and gazing down in wonderment at the rushing waters. At length, on this auspicious day of the third month, they reached the stone bridge that spanned the torrent. They were spellbound by the beauty of the scene beneath them: flowers all in bloom, hanging entwined with leaves in silken canopies, clear waters sparkling like silver, birds each outdoing the other with their beautiful melodies, gentle breezes recalling glad memories.

The eight fairies were delighted. They sat enchanted on the bridge, looking down at their reflections where the streams met in the sparkling crystal pool. Their delicate brows and radiant faces were mirrored in the water like a classical painting done in a master's hand, and they were so captivated they had no thought of moving on until the sun descended into the western mountains and the day grew dark.

At this very same moment Hsing-chen had crossed Tung-t'ing Lake and was entering the Underwater Palace. The Dragon King, full of gladness at his coming, personally came to the gate to greet him. He took the young monk by the hand and led him to his throne, which he bid him to share.

When Hsing-chen had made his obeisance and recited the message from his Master, the Dragon King bowed low in return. He commanded that a welcome feast be prepared—a splendid repast of fruits and delicacies of the kind known only to those who dwell among the mountains—and he personally offered Hsing-chen the wine, repeatedly urging him to drink.

But Hsing-chen refused the cup time and again. "Your Highness, this humble monk cannot partake of the wine," he said. "Wine unbalances and overstimulates the mind, and so it is strictly forbidden by the Buddha."

"I know that wine is among the five things that Gautama forbade," replied the Dragon King, "but this wine I offer is altogether different from the intoxicant that mortals drink. This wine calms the passions and quiets the mind. Surely, you do not doubt my intentions in offering it to you."

In the face of such generosity, Hsing-chen could not refuse. He drank three cups, said his goodbyes, and left the Underwater Palace, riding the wind directly to Lotus Peak.

When he lighted there, the power of the wine was already obvious on his face, and he was overcome by dizziness. "Master will be shocked if he sees me this way," he said to himself. "He will reprimand me most severely."

Crouching by the bank of a stream, he took off his robes and placed them on the clean sand. He dipped his hands in the clear water and was washing his hot face, when suddenly he noticed a strange and mysterious scent wafting toward him. It was not the fragrance of orchid, or musk, or some exotic flower—it was something entirely new to him, something he had never before experienced. The scent seemed to dissolve in him all tinges of passion and uncleanness, leaving him with a feeling of ineffable purity. "What fantastic flowers must be growing by the stream to exude such sweet perfume into the air," he thought. "I must investigate its source."

He dressed carefully and followed the course of the stream upwards, and there, quite suddenly, he found himself face-to-face with the eight fairies who were sitting on the stone bridge.

Hsing-chen put down his pilgrim's staff and bowed deeply as he addressed them. "Ladies of the Fairy Realm, please hear what I have to say, though I am but a poor monk. I am a disciple of the Great Master Liu-kuan and I live on Lotus Peak. I am now on my way back from a mission on which the Master sent me beyond the mountains. This bridge is not wide, and by sitting upon it, you are blocking my way. Dear goddesses, would you kindly move aside upon your lotus feet and let me pass?"

The fairies returned his bow. "We are attendants to Queen Wei, and we are on our way back from delivering greetings to your Master. We have paused here to rest awhile. Is it not written in *The Book of Rites*, concerning the law of the road, that the man goes to the left and woman to the right? Since this bridge is very narrow, and we are already sitting here, is it not proper for you to avoid it altogether and cross at some other place?"

"But the water is deep," Hsing-chen replied. "There is no other way to cross. Where do you suggest this humble monk should go?"

"It is said that the great Bodhidharma crossed the ocean on a single leaf," said the fairies. "If you are, in fact, a disciple of Master Liu-kuan and you have studied the Dharma with him, then surely you must have acquired some supernatural powers. It should not be hard for you to cross this tiny rivulet, so why do you stand there arguing with women over the right of way?"

Hsing-chen laughed. "I see from your attitude that you require some sort of payment for the right to cross, but I have no money. I am only a poor monk. Yet I have do have eight jewels, which I will happily give to you if you will permit me to pass." With this he plucked eight peach blossoms from a tree, held them between his palms, and tossed them before the fairies. What landed at their feet were four pairs of scarlet flowers, and these transformed into eight sparkling jewels that radiated their brilliant light high into to the heavens.

The eight fairies laughed with delight. Each of them rose from her place and lifted a scarlet flower, gave Hsing-chen a coy glance, mounted the wind, and sailed away through the air.

Hsing-chen stood at the bridge and watched for a long time until they were lost in the clouds and their sweet fragrance had melted away. He felt a terrible loneliness and dejection come over him, as if he had failed in his highest aspirations. And that is how he returned to the temple and delivered his message from the Dragon King.

When the Master reprimanded him for his late return Hsing-chen said, "The Dragon King treated me so generously, Master, it was impossible for me to refuse his kind request that I stay awhile. That is why I have been delayed."

The Master did not reply to this. He said, simply, "Go away and rest."

Hsing-chen went back to his meditation cell as the shadows of evening descended upon the day. Since he had seen the eight fairies, his ears had been echoing with their sweet voices, and he could not forget their beautiful faces and willowy forms. Try as he might, he found it impossible to control the thoughts that raced through his mind—he felt as if he were part drunkard and part madman. But he calmed himself and sat in his posture on the mat. He said to himself: "If a youth diligently studies the Confucian classics and serves his country as a minister of state or a general when he is grown into a man, he may dress in silks with an official seal upon his belt. He may serve the king, dispense favors among the people, look upon beauty with the eyes, and listen to sounds that delight the ears. He may have his fill of fame in this life and leave a legacy for future generations. But Buddhists have only a small bowl of rice and a jug of water. We study our dry tomes and count our *mala* beads until our hair goes white. It is a lofty and admirable religion, but the pit of vain desires it leaves unfulfilled is unspeakably deep. Though I may come to understand all the scriptures of the Mahayana path, though I may take the bodhisattva's vow and rise to the exalted position of sage and master, once my mind and spirit dissolve into smoke and nothingness, who will know that a person called Hsing-chen ever lived upon this earth?"

His thoughts wandered; he tried to sleep, but sleep refused to come; the hour grew late. When he closed his eyes for a moment, the eight fairies appeared before him all in a row and drove away all thoughts of sleep. It suddenly occurred to him that the great purpose of Buddhism was to tame the mind and the heart. "I have been a monk for ten years," he said, "and I had nearly succeeded in overcoming the world of craving, but now my treacherous mind has gotten entangled in desire, much to the detriment of my soul."

He burned incense, knelt, stilled his thoughts, and was counting his *mala* beads, visualizing the thousand Buddhas that could help him, when suddenly one of the temple boys came to his window and said, "Brother, are you asleep? The Master is calling you."

Hsing-chen was alarmed. "It is unusual for him to call me in the middle of the night. It must be something serious," he thought.

He followed the boy to the Hall of the Buddha, where all the monks of the temple had been assembled. The Master himself was sitting in solemn silence, brilliantly lit by the light of many candles. His appearance inspired both fear and curiosity, and when he spoke it was with great care, with grave intonation.

"Hsing-chen! Do you know how you have sinned?"

Hsing-chen was kneeling before the dais. He bowed low, until his head touched the floor, and he said, "Master, I have been your disciple for more than ten years now. I have never disobeyed a command. Nor have I failed to follow any order concerning our practice, in which I have had a part. I know only that I am dark with ignorance—I do not know what offense I have committed."

"There are three things that must be disciplined in one's practice—the body, the mind, and the soul. When you went to the Dragon King, you drank wine, did you not? And on your return, by the stone bridge, you flirted at length with the messengers of Queen Wei. You gave them each a flower, joked with them, and spoke frivolously. And since your return, you have not put the memory of those events from your heart and mind. Instead, you have allowed yourself to be entangled by worldly desires, pre-occupying yourself with riches and honor and all the other worldly temptations. You have turned away with distaste from the teachings of the Buddha, and thus your three degrees of at-tainment have all fallen from you in a single hour! You may no longer remain here."

Hsing-chen wept and pleaded for forgiveness. "Great Master," he said, "I have indeed sinned, but I was forced to break the rule that forbids drinking because the Dragon King compelled me. I talked with the fairies only because I was asking them to move out of the way. I had no ill intentions in my heart. How can you condemn me like this? I will return to my cell. Though impure thoughts tempt me with madness, I will keep my mind alert and overcome them. Surely, my true spirit will return. I will bite my hands and repent of the wrongs I have done, and my true heart will be restored. Does it not say in the teachings of Confucius that one can thus return to the right path? If I have done wrong, my most honorable Father, give me a flogging and set me right. Is that not according to the teaching of the Buddha? How could you banish me from all possibility of reform? I came to you when I was only twelve, I gave up my parents and relatives, I cut my hair and took refuge as a monk. Since then I have lived as your dependant, as if you yourself had begotten and raised me. The love between us is like that of a father and his only son. My cell is my sanctuary in this temple, and that is where my hopes all lie. Where else am I to go?"

"It is your desire to leave, and that is what makes me send you away," said the Master. "If that were not so, what could ever make me cast you out of this place? You ask, 'Where else am I to go?' My answer is simple: 'Go to the place you desire.'"

Then, Master Liu-kuan shouted, "Come, constables!" and suddenly they materialized from the thin air—the yellow-hatted Emissaries of Hell. They bowed and awaited his orders. "Take this man into your custody," said the Master. "Remove him to the Underworld and hand him over to Lord Yama, then come back and make your report to me."

When Hsing-chen heard this he felt as if his spirit had left him. His eyes overflowing with tears, he fell upon the floor, crying, "Father! Father, please! Listen to what I have to say! In ancient times the Great Master Ananda broke all the laws of the Buddha when he visited the house of a prostitute and had intercourse her. But the noble Shakyamuni did not condemn him! He embraced Ananda and showed him the Dharma ever more clearly. I may have transgressed, but compared to Ananda, surely I am less guilty! How can you send me to Hell?"

"When Ananda fell into sin, his mind was repentant," Master Liu-kuan replied. "You, on the other hand, have lost your heart and mind upon a single glimpse of those seductive creatures. Your thoughts have turned toward a life of pleasure. Your mouth waters for worldly honor and wealth. You fare badly in a comparison with Ananda. You cannot escape the grief and suffering that await you, Hsing-chen!"

Hsing-chen could not imagine leaving, and he continued to cry for mercy until the Master finally relaxed his sternness and comforted him. "Hsing-chen, while your mind is impure, you will never attain enlightenment, even up here in the mountains," he said. "But do not forget the Dharma. Hold true to it, and though you may mingle with dirt and impurities along the way, your return is assured. If it is ever your desire to return, Hsing-chen, then I shall go myself to bring you back, so do not doubt or question me. Now, go!"

There was nothing more to be said. Hsing-chen bowed low before the Master, said good-bye to his fellow monks, and went with the Emissaries of the Underworld.

They transported him, beyond the Lookout Pavilion, to the outer walls of Hell, and when the guards at the gate asked the cause of their coming, they said, "We have arrested this guilty man and bring him here at the orders of the Great Master Liu-kuan!" The guards opened the gates of Hell and let them through, into the inner court, where they once again announced their arrival.

And it was Yama himself, Lord of the Underworld, who commanded that they bring him in. "Honored Sir," he said to Hsing-chen, "though you abide in the hills under Lotus Peak, your name already rests on the incense table before the great King Ksitigarbha. I have thought to myself that in the future, when you ascend the Lotus Throne, all sentient creatures of the earth will be greatly blessed. So how is it that you have been arrested and dragged here before me in disgrace?"

Hsing-chen was confused and humiliated, and he did not reply for a long time. Finally, he said, "I met Queen's Wei's fairy maidens on the stone bridge of South Peak. I failed to restrain my carnal thoughts about them. I have sinned against my Master, and now, Your Majesty, I await your command."

Lord Yama sent a messenger to King Ksitigarbha with the following note:

> The Great Master Liu-kuan of Lotus Peak has sent me one of his disciples, escorted by the Yellow Hats. We are to come to a judgment, here in the Underworld, as to his guilt. Since his case is not like that of ordinary offenders I asking your High Majesty's council.

King Ksitigarbha replied:

> Each man has his own path to perfection, and each is reborn in order to carry out the things necessary to fulfill his karma. No man can escape the cycle of samsara, and therefore there is no point in our discussing this case.

Lord Yama was just about to come to a decision when two demon soldiers announced that the yellow-hatted Emissaries, by Master Liu-kuan's commannd, had brought eight more criminals, who were now waiting outside the gate. Hsing-chen was greatly alarmed.

Lord Yama commanded that they be brought in—and *behold!*—the eight fairy maidens of the Southern Peak came haltingly through the gate and knelt down in the court. "Listen, fairy maidens of South Peak!" said Yama. "You fairy folk live in the most beautiful of known worlds. You enjoy uncountable pleasures and delights. How is it that you come to this place?"

Greatly shamed, they replied in a babble of voices: "Our Mistress, Queen Wei, ordered us to pay a visit to the Great Master Liu-kuan to ask after his health and well being. On our way back to the Southern Peak, we met his disciple Hsing-chen. Because we talked with his disciple, Master Liu-kuan said that we had defiled the sacred laws of the mountains, and he wrote you to ask that we be banished to the Underworld. All our hopes are with your

Majesty, and we pray that you have mercy on us and allow us to
go back to the world of the living."

Lord Yama then called nine Emissaries, and they appeared
before him. In a deep voice, he commanded, "Take these nine and
return them at once to the world of the living."

He had hardly finished his pronouncement when a great
whirlwind arose and carried the nine off into the void, where they
were swirled apart and flung into the eight directions. Hsing-chen
was borne along by the wind, hurled and tossed in endless space
until, at last, he seemed to land on solid ground.

When the storm calmed, Hsing-chen gathered his wits about
him and found himself among a range of mountains bordered by a
beautiful, clear river. Below him was a bamboo grove, and beyond
that, through the shady branches of the trees, he could see a dozen
houses with thatched roofs. Several people were gathered there,
talking together within his earshot. "How marvelous it is!" they
said. "The hermit Yang's wife is past her fiftieth year, and yet she
is going to have a child! We have been waiting for a long time, but
have yet to hear the infant's cry. These are anxious moments."

Hsing-chen said to himself: "I will be reborn into the world of
humans. I can see that I am only a spirit now, for I have no body. I
left it on Lotus Peak. It has been cremated already, and I am so
young I have no disciples to recover my relics and keep them
safe."

As these ruminations about the past filled him with grief, one
of Yama's Emissaries appeared and motioned him over. "This is
the Hsiu-chou township of Huai-nan province in the empire of
T'ang," he said. "And here is the home of the hermit Yang, who is
your father. This is his wife, Liu, your mother. It is your karma to
be reincarnated in this household, so go quickly. Do not miss this
auspicious moment!"

Hsing-chen went in at once, and there sat the hermit wearing
his reed hat and a coat of rough hempen cloth. He was preparing
some sort of medicine on a brazier in front of him, and the
fragrance filled the house. From the room came the indistinct
moaning of someone in pain. "Go in quickly. Now!" the Emissary

urged again. When Hsing-chen continued to hesitate, the messenger gave him a hard push from behind.

Hsing-chen fell to the ground and instantly lost consciousness. It seemed that he had been propelled into some great natural cataclysm. "Help!" he cried. "Save me!" but the sounds caught in his throat, inarticulate, until they became the cries of an infant.

The midwives quickly announced to the hermit that his wife had borne him a beautiful son, and Yang took her the medicinal drink he had prepared. They looked at each other, their faces full of joy.

Hsing-chen was suckled when he was hungry, and he ceased his crying when he was satisfied. As a newborn he still recalled the events of his previous life on Lotus Peak, but as he grew older and knew of the love of his parents, the memories of his former existence faded away, and soon they were entirely forgotten.

When the hermit saw how handsome and talented he was, he stroked the child's little brow and said, "Indeed, you are a gift from Heaven come to dwell among us." And so he named him Shao-yu, meaning "Small Visitor," and gave him the special name Ch'ien-li, meaning "A Thousand *Li*."

Time passes like flowing water, and in what seemed the space of moments, the boy grew to be ten years old. His face had the quality of jade and his eyes shone bright as the Morning Star. He was strong, and his mind pure and bright, showing that he was most certainly a Superior Man. The hermit said to his wife, "I do not originally come from this world, but because I am with you I have dwelt among the dust of this earth in this mortal form. The devas who live on Mount P'eng-lai have called upon me many times to return to them. But because of your hard work and your suffering, I have refused them. Now Heaven has blessed us with a son who shows great talents, who is superior to others in his attainments. You may rely on him now, and in your old age you will surely enjoy wealth and honor through his achievements. Therefore, I need no longer delay my departure."

One day the devas came to escort him, some riding on white deer and some on blue herons, and they flew off together toward the distant mountains. Though a letter would come from time to time out of the clear blue sky, no traces of the hermit Yang were ever seen on this earth again.

◊

Grieving for Yin Yao

How long is a man's life
Before he returns to emptiness?
As I think of you, on the verge of death,
10,000 things trouble my heart.

Your mother not yet buried,
Your daughter only ten,
And yet from the far, cold, wilderness,
Already the sounds of mourning.

Clouds drift across an empty sky,
The birds are flying songless;
The way of the wanderer is lonely—
Even the sun goes pale and cold.

I am sorry—when you lived
And asked me to explain the Dharma,
My teachings came too late.
And in the end, it was all vanity.

Your old friends have brought you gifts,
But mine were too late for you in life.
I have failed you in so many ways,
I weep and close my gate of twigs.

—Wang Wei (701-761)

"This is myself and that is someone else" —
Free yourself from the constraints of such delusion
And your own self shall be awakened.

—Saraha, *The Treasury of Songs*

How Master Madman Came
to Ch'ing Feng Temple

*I*t is said that during the reign of Cheng Yuan (785-804 A.D.) of the
*T'ang Dynasty there lived in Chang-an a young man by the name of
Yang. He was just fifteen and yet learned far beyond his years. He
was graceful, his complexion clear, his eyes bright, his hair of fine luster.
He had the beauty, the grace, and the elegance of a girl, and yet he
conducted himself with the bearing of a warrior prince. He had about him
all the qualities of the superior man, and yet he had a terrible flaw: he was
proud, arrogant, and selfish. The official T'ang histories say that Yang
met a tragic end at the hands of barbarian bandits and that his younger
brother became a famous Royal Minister like their father.*

*But histories are always incomplete. This is the tale of how Yang
came to learn that he inhabited a world of delusion and began to seek the
virtues that would, in time, earn him the title "Master Anatman," also
known as "Master Madman." It is taken from a manuscript once housed
in the archives of the Collection of Antiquities at the National University
Library of Shanghai.*

◊

I.

It was springtime in the year of the Fire Horse. Icicles
dripped under the eaves of the tiled roofs, and where the water
splashed upon the ground, small pits appeared, dirt spattering in
dark rings. In the square of the inner courtyard white snow melted
along the tops of black branches, shimmering under the morning
sun.

And here young Master Yang, roused early from sleep, rubbed his eyes as he drank his morning tea. Today was the day he would meet his new tutor, an old monk widely renowned as a teacher of the ancient Buddhist scriptures, and a serving girl came to announce his arrival.

"Tell him to wait," said Yang, making no attempt to cover his nakedness under his open robe. The serving girl blushed and cast her eyes downward as she left the room. Yang took his time with breakfast and he made his dresser change his clothes twice. More than an hour passed before he finally emerged to meet the monk, and then he did not even bother to greet him or ask his name. "Why are you here so early?" he said.

The old monk bowed. "I have the honor of being your tutor, Young Master. Your father has no doubt told you that you are to study with me."

"If it were up to my father, I would study with every tutor and charlatan sage from here to India," said Yang, and though he knew full well, he asked, "What are you supposed to teach me?"

"According to your father's instructions, you are to accompany me to Ch'ing Feng Temple in the north. There I will instruct you in the sutras, the teachings of the Buddha."

"The sutras? I have no intention of becoming a monk. I will not shave my head or wear rags or eat the leftovers of households beneath mine."

"You need not become a monk, Young Master. You are to study the sutras as part of your education."

"And why must I go with you? Why can't we do it right here?"

"To properly study the sutras, we must go where they are housed, to a temple. We must hear how properly to chant them, and that requires that we be in the company of the monks. That is why we will go to Ch'ing Feng Temple."

"If I am to go to a drafty old temple, I want to know what provisions my father has made for my comfort."

"He has made a large offering, Young Master. Your needs will all be met. Now, after breakfast tomorrow, you will come with me."

"I will go with you, but not without my personal servants."

"As you know," said the monk, "many of the teachings are secret and privileged. Were you not such a prodigious scholar already, and had your father not made a substantial donation to the temple, I would not have been sent here by the head of my order. But I have been instructed to teach you. Therefore I shall, but it must be according to the rules of my order. You may not bring your servants."

"Do you know who I am?" said Yang. "Do you know who my father is? Surely, you are joking and an exception is to be made for me."

"It was your father who has instructed that we abide by the rules. The temple is to make no exceptions for you. Otherwise, how would you gain authentic knowledge? Can one learn to swim by stepping halfway into a lake?"

"I have studied the Rites, the Histories, and the Songs. I studied more than you could imagine, old man. I would be better served to have a tutor instruct me on the *The Book of Changes*. My father is wasting my time with religion."

"Even Emperors do not consider religion to be a waste of time, Young Master. You are young. You must bow respectfully to the wisdom of your father. If not, you will bow involuntarily to his authority. Tomorrow, we will leave according to his wishes."

"Then let it be known between us and to your master that I accompany you against my will. My father will live to regret this stupidity." Yang made a show of ordering that his horse and travel clothes be prepared, though he knew that his father had already made all arrangements.

They set out the following morning shortly after dawn. It was an auspicious day, and Yang did not mind traveling on horseback along the dusty roads that led northward into the mountains. An entourage of his father's servants accompanied him that day, and they set up a lavish camp for the night. He dined on roast pig, exotic vegetables, and wild mushrooms taken from the high forest, and he was entertained by his father's favorite courtesan, who played odes and melancholy ballads on the silk-stringed *ch'in*. And after a dozen glasses of wine, poured for him by his father's favorite concubine, he fell into a stupor, having quite forgotten the old monk.

That night Yang dreamed he was a great general riding to battle in a gleaming war chariot armored in pure gold. He carried a bow that could lay waste to the enemy, for the arrows were magical—they could explode into flames, cause madness, shower down a rain of poisonous glass shards. Yang was confident. He was brave. The one-wheeled chariot—self-propelled, or perhaps drawn by invisible horses—sped into battle, and Yang was the hero, the first to engage the enemy. And in this dream the enemy was not human—they were a horde of cannibal demons wearing the armor of dead soldiers from the time of the First Emperor, carrying antiquated weapons, shouting war cries in their guttural tongues. They swarmed towards him like the foaming waves of the sea, and then, as he notched an arrow and drew back his magic bow, an odd thing happened. The dream split in two, each half playing over the other half, as if the two were superimposed one on top of the other. In one dream his magic arrows caused great confusion and panic, and then he drew his great sword and drove through the demons, mowing them down like a field of ripe wheat. But in the other dream the chariot suddenly stopped and would not move. The single wheel was stuck. There was something wrong with the eight spokes, something with how they converged on a point of nothingness. The demons were upon him like a ravenous swarm of locusts. He was overwhelmed by their stench of spoilt milk and rotting meat, the sight of their goggling round eyes, their red and yellow fur, their sickly white flesh like the bellies of dead fish. They tore him to pieces. And then a third dream superimposed itself over the first two: it was himself, waking up in his tent, covered in furs and silken blankets, sitting bolt upright in a cold sweat, mute, wide-eyed; and he woke at that moment, as if he had entered the dream world from another, unknown world.

Yang found himself in his bed. From the firelight outside the

tent, he could make out the sleeping forms of his father's con-
cubine and the servants. He heard a horse snort. He got up, drew
on his robe, and walked out into the starlit night.

The old monk was awake—or appeared to be. He sat near the
fire counting his wooden prayer beads, which were alternately red
and black, made of cherry and ebony.

"Do you have a cure for indigestion?" Yang asked him. "I have
just woken from a terrible dream."

"Do not overeat, and do not eat what is not easily digested,"
said the monk.

"Useless," said Yang. "What you say prevents indigestion. It
offers no remedy." He let out a foul belch. "I ate too much because
I know I will starve up there at your temple. Get some sleep, old
man. You will need your strength tomorrow."

Yang went back into his tent and slept fitfully, trying to figure
out why the wheel of his chariot would not turn. Perhaps I should
have asked the old man, he thought as he drifted off.

2.

In the morning they left the entourage behind, taking only
one pack horse to carry Yang's many necessities and a mule for the
monk to ride. There was much moaning and crying among the
servants, which Yang knew was all an act, but which he humored
for his own pleasure. He and the monk continued alone.

They needed no protection, the monk had assured him,
because like the fabled Hsuan Tsang, who had journeyed to India
for the scriptures, they were under the divine protection of the
Buddha. And the monk would draw on his own powers if the
need arose.

The monk was taciturn, but Yang today was excited by the
prospect of learning Buddhist magic, and when he learned that the
monk had been to Tibet, he asked question after question. "Which
is the easiest to learn?" he asked. "I have heard that in Tibet one of
the first spells is the spell of psychic heat that allows a man to sleep

in a cave with no blanket, even in the middle of a blizzard. Is it true that they can dry a dozen sheets soaked in icy water in winter just by the power of their thoughts?"

"It is true," said the monk.

"Is it true that they have a way of running that takes them a hundred *li* in a matter of minutes? And leaving no footprints even upon muddy ground? And that they may simply project a ghost double of themselves to send a message to a faraway town?"

"It is true."

"Which will I learn first? What would you recommend?"

"I could not tell you, young Master. I am only to be your tutor for the sutras."

"But surely, you can teach me a little magic. Isn't that part of a monk's training? Can you push your palm against solid stone and leave the print of your hand? I have heard that great monks can do that. Have you learned how?"

"No, I have not."

"Have you seen it?"

"I have not. But I have heard of such feats."

"And what about levitation? Have you seen levitation?"

"I have not."

"Then you must be a lowly monk and your temple must be unremarkable," said Yang. "Tell me, monk, are you an *arhat*? Are you enlightened?"

"I am not," said the monk. "It is what I aspire to. And yet were I to reach the gates of Nirvana, I would come back to this world to help others reach it before me. That is the vow of our order."

"What a foolish vow," said Yang. "That would be like a starving man finally reaching the banquet table and then allowing everyone else to eat first. Utter foolishness."

"We strive to achieve enlightenment—to end the cycle of birth and rebirth in a world of suffering. Not merely for ourselves, but for all beings in the world."

"I see that as a great waste of one's life, monk. First, the world is not all suffering. My life is full of enjoyment. Do you enjoy yourself?"

"The cause of enjoyment is also the cause of suffering. And the self is an illusion."

Yang laughed. "The self is an illusion?" He pinched himself and let out a mock cry of pain. "Enjoyment and suffering of the same cause? You Buddhists are an interesting lot."

"In time you will understand."

"I'm sure I will," said Yang. He laughed again.

They had arrived at an ancient gravesite—a dolmen made of two giant stones supporting a cracked slab like a table above them. Around the dolmen was a ring of smaller stones partially buried in the earth. Yang could make out the ashes and stones of an old fire pit and the debris of many camps.

"What is this place?" he asked.

The monk touched his prayer beads and made a gesture whose meaning Yang did not know. "It is a bad place," he said. "There are demons here who prey on passers by. Let us move on without disturbing them."

"I'm tired," said Yang. "And I see that many people have stopped here. It is clearly not dangerous. Don't you Buddhists consider the old religions mere superstition?"

"Let us go a little father until we leave these woods," said the monk. "Then we may rest where it is safe."

Yang wheeled his horse impatiently. "Fine. And how much farther?"

Before the monk could answer, there came a loud shout from the hillside, then the thunder of hoofbeats. Yang turned and saw a dozen horses galloping toward them—small horses of the barbarian breed. "Bandits!" he cried.

"Do not run!" called the monk. "They want only your money, but if you try to escape they will hunt you down for sport!"

Yang considered the monk's words. He looked at the old man in his coarse gray robe and then at his own embroidered silks, the old man's wooden beads and his own gold and silver. He saw the bandits riding down the hillside on their fast ponies, their unruly clothes, their shaggy beards and pockmarked faces. Their leader wore a fur hat of the horse clans and sported a red scar that split his face diagonally from brow to chin. Yang could almost smell the filth on his greasy furs. He looked at the monk to catch his eye, and then, with a flick of his whip, Yang wheeled his mount and galloped off down the trail, knowing the barbarian ponies could never catch his racehorse. He rode mercilessly, better than he imagined he could, his fear giving him strength and speed. He whipped his horse until his arm hung limp from exhaustion and he rode on still, spurring and spurring until the horse collapsed beneath him and he tumbled to the ground.

He did not know where he was or how long he had been riding. An eerie silence had settled around him—except for the wet, rasping breath of the horse. Its mouth was spewing bloody spittle and it stared at him with its frightened, terribly wide eyes, trying vainly to raise itself from the ground.

Yang dusted off his clothes. He was not injured. But the horse had broken one of its front legs and the bone protruded like a large sliver of birch wood. It sickened him. He knew that the proper thing to do was to kill the horse, but he could not bear it—not the gruesomeness, not the inconvenience. That was for a servant—or a butcher. And the wolves will be here to finish him off, he thought. They will smell the blood and come here. Let them be distracted by the horse. The thought of wolves frightened Yang. Quickly, he took the saddle blanket and his saddle pack, and he made his way into the darkening woods. Behind him he could hear the plaintive sounds of the horse—pathetic, disgusting. A little later, as clouds blackened the horizon, he heard the first wolf's howl.

3.

The house was not yet a ruin, but it had been abandoned for a long time. The gate still hung on iron hinges black with rust. The wood, once colorful with paint, was now a dull gray and what remained of the nameplate was only the single character of the surname: Li. The courtyard was overgrown in mugwort and tall grasses; once-tended trees had grown wild in the garden orchard now thick with weeds. The place made Yang imagine what his father's house might look like in a hundred years if his family fell out of favor with the Emperor. He felt a strange sensation in the pit of his stomach.

Yang went to the gate and called out, several times, but got no answer. He waited until he knew no one would answer, and then he opened the bare wooden gate on its shrieking hinges and entered the courtyard. It was a wealthy house, paved in stone, but now tufts of dry grass and dead weeds poked through the cracks. Everything was bleak and colorless, the paper panels in tatters, the lattices skeletal, metal fixtures tarnished or rusted black. Once again, he called out and heard not even an echo in reply.

In most of the rooms the ceiling had collapsed altogether or there were gaping holes through which Yang could make out the stars and the moon. He went from room to room until he found one past the inner courtyard—a receiving room set up like the one in which his father conducted his official business. Here the beams were sound and the ceiling undamaged. It was warmer, too, though Yang could still feel the breeze blowing in through the broken shutters. This is where he would spend the night. He looked for the warmest corner, where he might move a piece of furniture and sleep on it to avoid the cold stone floor. And he wept out of frustration and from the sheer hardship of it all. Only that morning he had been surrounded by his father's servants. He had woken in a warm and comfortable bed, enjoyed hot tea and a dainty breakfast while he still lounged in his sleep robe. These memories brought back images so vivid that he could smell them—the subtle fried odors, the light touch of spices, the warm steam of the tea upon his face. His stomach rumbled with hunger, his limbs ached with exhaustion. He huddled as best he could and sobbed himself to sleep.

He awoke late that night. The moon he had seen through the broken ceilings now shone low through the western windows. It was clear, nearly white in the cloudless night. But it was not the light, with its bluish caste, that had woken him. It was a noise— someone grunting, footsteps, the sound of something heavy being dragged. And then he saw it—a demon, a tall and lanky black demon dragging the body of a dead man.

Though Yang, like all well-bred young men, had been taught the martial arts and the ways of swordsmanship, he was a coward and now feared for his own life. He clasped a hand over his mouth lest he make a sound. He stood motionless until he was sure the demon had not seen him, and then he quietly crept backwards to hide behind a pile of broken furniture.

The demon, grunting and grumbling, pulled the body into the room. Drool leaked from his lower lip where his yellow fangs protruded like boars' tusks. Yang could smell him—or was it the odor of decay from the corpse? And now as the demon passed across a patch of moonlight, Yang recognized the body. It was the fat bearded man, the leader of the bandits still wearing his fur hat. The demon dragged him so close Yang could see the scar on the bandit's face, the gash on his neck, the black, clotted blood, the wide-open eyes, the bloated, protruding tongue.

The demon cursed and spat. He squatted on his haunches, facing the far door, and leaned over the bandit's body, prodding at the belly. He was unhappy about something. He grunted again and squatted back down by the bandit's head. He was naked— what Yang had taken to be the dangling end of a belt was actually the demon's penis. It was so long it flopped on the floor, oozing urine from its puckered foreskin. In a moment Yang could smell the acrid stench.

Now the demon sighed, turning his head to glance out of the window at the moon. He had three red eyes, and Yang, though he trembled with fear, could not help but be fascinated by how they blinked alternately so that two were always open. Without looking down, the demon casually jabbed one of its long thumbnails into the corpse's left eye socket and gouged out an eyeball. It was surprisingly large—twice the size Yang imagined an eye must be. Perhaps it had swollen in death. The demon popped the eye into his mouth and bit down. Liquid squirted as the eyeball burst like a ripe grape. There was a bright shimmer on the floor where the fluid reflected the moonlight.

Yang could not help himself—his gorge rose in his throat, and it was only by sheer force of will that he kept from vomiting. He felt a dry heave, like a hiccup, then another, and he was calm again. He closed his eyes and did not see the demon's ears twitch and its nostrils flare.

After a little while the demon got up and stalked out of the room. Yang knew he had to escape, but he dared not move until he knew it was safe. What if the demon was still near enough to hear him? He must wait, but then what if he waited too long and the demon returned? If he could wait until daylight he was sure to be safe, but he had no sense of the time and did not know how long it would be until sunrise. His heart was pounding. He was covered in sweat. He grew more anxious with each passing minute until it was fear and not bravery that made him resolve to get up.

But it was too late. The demon had returned. No—it was another demon, a red-skinned monster with a narrow chest and distended belly, with one crooked tusk and the other broken. It crept in looking left and right, approaching cautiously until it stood over the bandit's corpse. This one also poked the corpse's belly so hard that Yang could hear a sound, like someone breaking wind, and then he saw a black fluid leaking from the leg of the bandit's fur pants. And now he smelled the stench of rot and excrement. Yang wrinkled his nose and covered his face with his sleeve.

The red demon lifted the corpse and slung it over his shoulder, letting out a loud grunt of exertion. But before it could move, a gravelly voice barked, "Stop!" The red demon looked toward the far door. It was the black demon.

"He's mine! Put him down or I'll gut you where you stand!"

"I found him first," said the red demon. "He's mine."

The black demon pointed at the corpse. "I brought him here. If you doubt me, look at his face and you'll see I've already plucked out an eye."

Turning his head so he could make out the corpse's face, the red demon asked, "Which eye?"

The black demon hesitated. "The right eye. No! The left! No!

To the Nine Hells with you—how should I remember which eye?"

"Then he is mine," the red demon sneered.

"Wait! I ate it. Come kiss me and you will still taste its flavor on my lips!"

"I'd rather lick a pig's ass," said the red demon. "He's a big one. Let's share him, then."

"I'll have what's mine!" said the black demon. "Put him down before I lose my patience." He rose to his full height and spread his arms wide. The muscles of his chest rippled under his mangy fur.

The red demon dropped the corpse but he did not retreat. Instead, he reached into the shadows and produced a large club studded with metal spikes, and this he lifted high and slammed down onto the floor, showering the room with sparks and chips of stone. A stone splinter hit Yang on the cheek, drawing blood.

"Not so fast," said the black demon. "Since we can't agree, let us have an impartial observer judge our case."

"What impartial observer?" said the red demon, eyeing the corpse. "This one's got only one eye, and he's dead."

"Not him," said the black demon. "Him!" And he pointed directly at Yang where he cowered behind a bed.

"Who?" The red demon turned, and now both were looking at Yang with their round fiery eyes.

There was no point in trying to hide any longer. Yang stood on trembling legs feeling queasy and light-headed. He had heard of fear turning a man's bowels to water and he had not understood. Now he felt as if his insides would come splashing down at his feet.

"Who are you?" said the red demon.

Yang's mouth felt as if it were stuffed with raw cotton. Only a croaking sound came from his throat when he tried to answer.

"What does it matter who he is?" said the black demon. "Let us each present our case and let him decide who gets the meat. I could rip you limb from limb, but I'd rather not spill the blood of my own kind in a quarrel over food."

"Limb from limb, you say? I could bat your head from here to Loyang, but I shall spare you because our little judge will see things my way."

"Very well," said the black demon. He grabbed Yang and placed him on a stool on top of the broken furniture. Then he presented his case, describing how he and his brothers had been disturbed that day by a group of bandits dividing their loot in front of their home among the dolmens. They had killed most of the bandits and then they had fought over the meat. He had lost the horses and the mule but had managed to get two men. "They had a hostage—an old monk. But he was too skinny—a vegetarian, no doubt," the demon said. "But this one was meaty and plump, so I dragged him up here to eat in peace where my brothers would not disturb me. I left him to ripen a bit and went back for the monk—they say a monk's brain is especially sweet from having pure thoughts. But the monk was gone! Stolen! Then I come back to find him making off with my meat!" The black demon gestured contemptuously at the red demon, who merely snorted.

"Quite a tale," said the red demon. "And perhaps it is even true. But it is irrelevant."

"What?" said the black demon. "How can the truth be irrelevant? You! Are you mute? Ask him!"

Yang cleared his throat. From where he sat above them he could see the black demon's fur standing on end. He was furious. Indeed, Yang realized that however he judged the case, one of the demons was bound to be angry and would probably eat him. Or perhaps this was all a cruel charade they were performed for their own perverse demonic amusement, knowing all along that they would end up sharing the meat of the two humans. I am dead, thought Yang. Of that I am certain, and only the particular time and circumstances are not yet known to me. They will kill me and devour my flesh. My eyeballs will burst between their teeth. They will rip me to pieces, break open my bones, suck out my marrow.

The black demon's slap brought Yang out of his reverie. "I said ask him! How can the truth be irrelevant? You are the judge, so judge!"

Yang coughed, and he spoke without thinking. "I will judge fairly," he said. "But first I must have your assurance that you will let me go free."

Both demons laughed until their fangs were flecked with spittle. "My assurance!" said the black demon. "You want my assurance? You have it! I'll rip your head from your neck and use your skull as a chamber pot if you don't pass your judgment now!"

Yang realized that the black demon expected the judgment to be in his favor. The demon had probably noticed him when he had first come with the bandit's corpse. Or had he? If he had known all along, why hadn't the demon simply eaten him then instead of leaving the corpse behind and allowing him a chance to escape? Yang could not make sense of it. But now his understanding of his own death had become a cold certainty, and he began to wonder how he would meet that death. The demons would not let him live. He was a dead man. He thought of his father the Minister, his family name, the honor of his ancestors. At least he could die with honor.

And so Yang decided that if he were to die, it would be with dignity. He would tell the truth. He looked at the red demon. "Honorable demon," he said, "it may seem to you that you discovered an abandoned corpse, but I witnessed your colleague enter this room earlier in the evening. He did, in fact, eat an eye from the corpse. And when he left, it was not with the attitude of one abandoning one's property. I have been here since nightfall and I speak the truth."

"See," said the black demon. "Spoken like a magistrate!"

At first the red demon was quiet. He seemed resigned to the judgment. But he was oddly calm. "You speak the truth," he said. "But your truth is irrelevant. Why? Why is the truth irrelevant?" He turned to the black demon. "Because, my friend, you are in my house and what is left in my house is mine by law. What is more, you are both here without invitation. You are intruders. And I may exact a penalty for your rude trespassing if I so desire."

"What?" said the black demon. "What proof do you have that this house belongs to you?"

"And what proof do you have that the gravesite where you

live is the property of you and your brothers?"

"We've lived there for centuries among the dolmens," said the black demon.

"I have lived here for six turns of the zodiac," said the red demon, reaching for the bandit's corpse.

"Wait," said Yang.

The red demon paused.

"What is your surname?"

"What? I am a demon. I have no surname, only the names by which I am feared and loathed. Would you like to hear some of them?"

"No," said Yang. "But this house is owned by the family of Li according to the nameplate. And unless you have purchased this property from them through a proxy and such purchase is recorded in the archives of the Assessor, this house cannot be yours. By law, no demon or ghost may own property."

"You're just a damned squatter!" said the black demon. "Now get your hands off my meat!"

The red demon was quiet again. But in his silence, Yang saw that his fur bristled and ropy veins pulsed at his temples. "A corrupt judgment!" he cried. "Fraud!"

"Shut up and be on your way," said the black demon.

"Am I a dimwit? You believe I will lose one meal and simply leave you with yet another? Ha!"

The black demon strode forward and stood over the bandit's corpse.

"Go ahead and eat your pig," said the red demon. "I shall have the lamb over there."

The red demon moved so quickly that Yang saw not even a blur. But he felt a horrific blow, as if he had been hit by the side of a mountain, and then his entire body burned with a pain so fierce he could not even hear his own scream. His vision went white, then dimmed, then filled with sparks of light. But the most awful thing was the sound of it—like the gristly sound a drumstick makes when one rips it from a pheasant's hip, but louder, and with a force that shuddered through his entire body. Yang screamed, he doubled over, and when his vision cleared he saw his right arm—the glowing white bone of the shoulder joint—in the moonlight, the black, gushing of blood. He stood stupefied, as if he would at any moment wake from this unpleasant dream. But he did not wake. He felt, instead, for the ragged mess of his shoulder socket. He felt his hot blood spurt against his good hand. And then, in another instant, something hit him against the torn shoulder—so hard he fell to the floor with the wind knocked from his lungs. While Yang lay groaning and waiting to die, he heard the black demon cursing. The red demon dropped Yang's arm and cursed back. There was a strange tingling in Yang's right shoulder—like a thousand bristles poking him, and when he looked, he saw an arm attached there—the bandit's arm—bathed in a pale blue-white light. And now he though this was certainly a nightmare. He would endure it, surely, and he would awaken in his comfortable bed. Why else would his concern be so oddly out of place? Instead of fearing for his life, Yang was annoyed and angered at the thought of having to live with mismatched arms. The bandit's hands were coarse—his flesh was unpleasantly hairy and sunburnt. What an embarrassment to have to reveal such a limb in front of his servants. Yang closed his eyes and waited for the nightmare to be over.

But the red demon was still angry. He ripped Yang's other arm from its socket. And while Yang screamed again—shrill as a pig at slaughter—the black demon ripped the other arm from the bandit's corpse and attached it to Yang, affixing it there with the glowing life energy of *ch'i*. And then it happened with a leg, and the other leg. The pain was so great that Yang could no longer feel it, and now he was even more certain it was all a nightmare. He was outside his body, looking down at himself as people are wont to do in times of great trauma. He saw the red demon jab his claw through his belly and rip out his intestines. He wondered how they could be so incredibly long. The red demon twirled his arm as length after slimy length slid out of Yang's belly and his innards all lay in one big steaming pile on the stone floor. The black demon looked indignant—he said something to the red demon, who laughed. But Yang could hear no sound. He watched, numb and helpless, as the black demon ripped open the bandit's belly and lifted out an armload of intestine, which he dropped onto the floor. And this continued, this perverse game, until his living body and the bandit's corpse were both as hollow as gutted birds ready for stuffing. The demons exchanged the empty torsos and the black demon refilled Yang's body with the pile of organs from the floor.

Yang was confused. Now all that remained of himself on his body was his head. Everything else was pieces taken from the bandit's corpse. Yang's original arms and legs, his organs, his empty torso—now all lay scattered on the floor. But surely, I am still me, he thought. While my head is intact, I am still myself. How, then, was he able to look at his body from outside, unless this was a dream? Or was it true what they said about how one's spirit could live independent from the body, how it could travel the world at night while the body lay in bed. And which was his real self then, the body or the spirit?

Now the red demon grabbed Yang with one hand on each side of the face, a thumb jammed so far into each ear that Yang felt his eardrums burst. The demon pulled him close and opened his fanged jaw, and at that moment Yang was back inside his body, seeing out of his own eyes the hideous round eyes of the red demon; he smelled the demon's fetid breath; he could hear the rasp of hot wind blowing from the demon's bull-like nostrils.

"Let him go," said the black demon.

"Who?" said the red demon, and he pressed his fat lips against Yang's nose and sucked, clasping his palm over Yang's mouth so he could not breathe.

Yang could make no sound against this strange kiss. He flailed at the demon with his arms, now muscular, which had once belonged to the bandit. He struggled, kicked his legs, but the demon did not let go, and in another moment Yang felt a horrific pressure as the red demon sucked his brain out through his nose and spat mouthfuls of it onto the floor, where it quivered like piles of thick mucus. At that, the black demon split open the dead bandit's skull and removed the coagulated brain, wrinkled like two huge, veined walnut halves. Yang closed his eyes as his head was ripped off by the red demon. When he opened them again a moment later, Yang was looking at his own head on the floor. He was looking out of the dead bandit's eyes, which were somehow his. But Yang's own body—all of it—now lay strewn across the floor in bloody pieces. Arms, legs, torso, entrails, brains, head. He had looked behind his father's kitchens once when he was a boy. It was the fall moon festival and the cooks had butchered dozens of pigs and cows. This is how the kitchen floor had looked—like a charnel house.

I am dead, thought Yang. There lies my body. But then how could he be seeing himself? My spirit is still alive, he thought. And he could feel his body—his new body, the corpse of the bandit. But how could he be alive if he were the dead body of another man? Was Yang dead, and he was the dead bandit come to life again? How could he not know whether he was alive or dead?

Now the demons were laughing. The red demon pointed at the gruesome mess on the floor and the black demon was nodding in agreement. They each picked up a severed leg—Yang's legs— and began to eat, their eyes rolling with pleasure. They were so preoccupied, eating so greedily, that they paid no heed when Yang—or the reanimated corpse of the bandit—finally made his escape.

4.

Several days later, the remaining bandits found their leader wandering in the woods. They were overjoyed to see him alive, for they had assumed him to be dead, but then they were terribly saddened to discover that he had lost his mind. He no longer recognized them or even knew his own name. He was covered in dried blood and his own filth. And he remembered nothing. When he could speak, they knew he was surely mad because he asked to be taken back to Chang-an to his father the Royal Minister. His tone of voice, his manner, his expression had all softened. He was almost effeminate.

Out of respect for their former leader, they took him to the Ch'ing Feng Temple and left him under the care of the monks. The bandits donated a large sum of gold, some of which they had taken from Yang's packhorse, and requested that the monks nurse their leader back to health. If his memory and sanity did not return, the monks were to humor him and tend to him as best they could until the time of his natural death. Though the bandits of the horse clans are said to be uncivilized, there is honor even among outlaws, and they had great sympathy for the horrors their leader must have suffered at the hands of the demons he had described.

On the evening of the bandits' departure, Master Lao Shan, the Abbot of Ch'ing Feng Temple, returned and the monks brought the madman to him to tell his improbable tale. To their great surprise, the two immediately recognized each other, and the Abbot asked the monks to leave them.

When they were alone, the madman kowtowed to the Master, sobbing and making abject apology. He told his story, and at the end he said, "Please, who am I? I have all the memories of my life as Yang, but how can that be me if I am in the body of this bandit, whom the other bandits say is their leader, Han Lung? They tell me I have lost my mind from the tortures the demons put me through. They say I must have fabricated all my memories of being Yang. Am I Han Lung, with no memory of my own past, with the absurd belief that I am the son of a Royal Minister? Please, Master, do you know who I am?"

"I recall that is what Yang said when we first met," said Lao Shan. "Tell me, who do you see when you look in the mirror?"

"I have looked in the mirror many times. So much that the bandits took it away from me. Each time, I see Han Lung. There is no mistake."

"And who is the I who sees Han Lung?"

There was a long pause. "Yang," said the madman. "Inside, I am Yang. Of that I am certain. Han Lung's body is what I occupy, but I know I am Yang."

"And yet a true madman would be entirely convinced of the

truth of his own delusions. What you say to me is precisely what the mad Han Lung would say."

"But Master, Han Lung was dead. How can I be a corpse brought back to life?"

"How can you be the consciousness of one man trapped in the corpse of another which was brought back to life? Each tale is equally fantastic. Which is more plausible? I will send you to Yang's father. Will he believe your story? Will he recognize your true identity?"

The madman wept. "I have pondered this for days until it drove me mad and then made me sane again. He will not. My father will rather believe that Han Lung murdered his son, having tortured out of him all the personal memories I would be likely to present as evidence that I am Yang."

"In fact," said Lao Shan, "I have just come from Chang-an, where Yang's father has already buried the bones of his son. They were found with his clothes in an abandoned house near the ancient dolmens."

The madman wept more loudly, pounding his breast and tearing at his hair.

"Yang's younger brother is now the heir. Is the Minister likely to believe in the miracle of his first son's survival in the body of a notorious criminal? Or would he, and the new heir, have Han Lung immediately arrested and put to death of the brutal murder of Yang?"

"Please, Master, I understand that whatever I may believe—whatever I may hold true within myself—what others see of me has more power to decide my identity than what I believe myself. But surely, you of all people must believe my story. You were there when the bandits attacked us. You warned me not to run. It was me—Yang—who abandoned you to the bandits. I did not know you were the great Master Lao Shan. I took you for a lowly monk. I am sorry for that. I am truly sorry."

"Let me ask you," said Lao Shan, "how do you know that I do not have a similar tale to tell? What if the demons perform this charade of theirs again and again for their amusement? What if I am actually the bandit Han Lung whose spirit was taken from his body before his death and put into the reanimated body of a dead old monk named Lao Shan? Could you know?"

The madman did not have to think long before he answered, "No. But all the monks here believe you to be their Master. You must be him."

"All the bandits believe you to be their leader, Han Lung. Must you not be him?"

"But they believe I am insane. The monks don't think that of you!"

"Perhaps Han Lung studied the sutras as a youth. Perhaps he was a monk before he became a bandit. Perhaps I am a better imposter than you."

The madman put his hands over his ears. "Please, Master," he begged as his tears darkened the wooden floor, "call me by a name. Call me Yang or call me Han Lung and that is who I shall be. If you do not save me, I will surely go mad again, and this time I will die."

"It is not in my power to decide who you are. I recall telling Yang that the cause of enjoyment and the cause of suffering were the same."

"Yes. I remember. You also said that the self is an illusion. Now I understand that pain and suffering both come from the self."

"And have you learned the nature of the self?"

The madman wept bitterly at those words, remembering how he had scoffed at the old monk. He cried for a long time, until there were no more tears. "I understand," he said finally. "I cannot go home. Let me stay here. You were to be my tutor for the sutras. I will stay to study the Buddha's teachings with you."

"And I will be honored to teach you whether you are Yang or Han Lung," said the Master.

◊

In the T'ang histories, it is said that the mad bandit Han Lung became a distinguished disciple of Master Lao Shan, but nothing is said about the nature of Han Lung's madness. Upon the Master's passing, Han Lung became Abbot of Ch'ing Feng Temple and was known officially as "Master Anatman," for by then he was widely renowned for his teaching of the doctrine of "no self." No details are given for why he was also called "Master Madman."

Even during the Ming Dynasty (1368-1643 A.D.), one could still view the prayer beads that Master Lao Shan had passed down to his successor. They were made of cherry and ebony wood and displayed on top of a folded ricepaper text at Ch'ing Feng Temple. It is said that Tang Yin, an early Ming scholar widely known for exposing unscrupulous practitioners of Taoist alchemy, transcribed the above tale from that text. (He is referred to in an anonymously-written cautionary narrative of the period called "The Alchemist and His Concubine.") Stylistic clues suggest that Tang Yin's text may have been later embellished by Wang Shih-cheng (1525-1590 A.D.) sometime after he wrote his scandalous novel, Gold Vase Plum.

Ch'ing Feng Temple was destroyed by fire under the Manchus in 1647.

◊

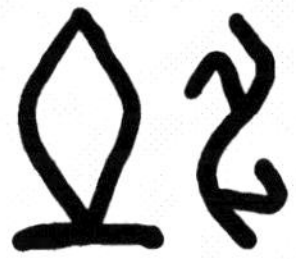

佳

If you are coming down through the narrows
           of the river Kiang,
Please let me know beforehand,
And I will come out to meet you
                              As far as Cho-fu-Sa.

                    —Li Po (701-762)
                       "The River Merchant's Wife:
                       A Letter"

Lament of the Farm Wife of Wu

This year the rice ripens bitterly late.
Soon we shall see the cold winds come,
And when the winds come cold the rains will pour,
The harrow-heads mold, the sickles rust.

Eyes dry and tears cease—but the rain is endless.
How can we bear the sight of those golden stalks crushed
    in green mud?

In a thatched hut for a month on the paddy's edge we lived.
The skies cleared. We harvested and followed the wagon home.
Sweat pouring and shoulders raw, we hauled the grain to market,
But the price was low. We gave it away like chaff.

"Sell the cow to pay the tax! Split the roof for firewood!"
These shallow plans won't get us far. Next year we starve.

Officials these days want cash—won't take rice any more.
In the Northwest, the Ten Thousand Li Frontier beckons
    the Chiang-er,
And though wise men fill the court, the people suffer more
    bitterly.
I'd rather be a river merchant's wife.

—Su Tung-p'o (1036-1101)

羽

Song Bird

In the summer of 2001, during my year off before tenure, I had the pleasure of visiting Vancouver under the pretext of attending an international Korean literature conference. I had been invited as a juror for a translation competition, but the real reason I went was to visit my old friend and colleague, Lew Waters. I had known him since 1984, when we were in Korea studying language and literature as Fulbright Scholars. I was there as a folklorist, and he was there to study modern poetry; we met in an intensive class at Yonsei University's Korean Language Institute and spent a great deal of time studying and drinking together. We were both in our twenties: young, irresponsible, and full of intellectual energy.

In late spring of 1985, Lew and I narrowly missed being held hostage when Korean university students took over the library of the United States Information Service for several days. This was before students had begun to immolate themselves to protest American policy in Korea (the way that Thich Quang Duc, the Vietnamese Buddhist monk, did in 1963—Malcolm Browne's photo burned into our collective memories); they had torched the U.S.I.S. library in Taegu, but the takeover in Seoul was well-coordinated and relatively peaceful—only a couple of Korean guards were manhandled. We offered the authorities our services as intermediaries to help with negotiations, since we were both students ourselves and therefore might have the trust of the Koreans, but the American State Department people had not been kindly disposed to dealing with mere "graduate students," even if we were there under the auspices of the Fulbright program. In retrospect, I realize they were concerned with our safety, but in those naive and idealistic days, neither of us would have believed it to be their true motivation. The person who had the unpleasant task of dealing with us was an American 8th Army colonel, and he is the one responsible for the story that took the next sixteen years to unfold.

Colonel Noakowski dealt with us with great patience and a detectable degree of condescension, but he was also good to us in an unexpected way. He happened to be related to the great Reverend Gale, the missionary who had done pioneering translation of Classical Korean texts in the last century, and so the Colonel had a certain soft spot for us. He took us onto the 8th Army compound in Yongsan, entertained us with a steak dinner at the Officer's Club, and even arranged, later, for us to take the tour of the notorious "Tunnels of Aggression" the North Koreans had dug under the DMZ. He confessed to us that he had acquired a taste for collecting antique Korean "knick-knacks," and his great delight was in showing us his personal study, in which he displayed a fantastic range of things whose true value was unknown to him: 16th century folk paintings of mountain gods and Taoist sages, panels from Buddhist temple walls, authentic masks from the T'alch'um, embroidered rank insignia from Yi Dynasty silk robes. Even with our amateur knowledge of Korean antiquities at the time, we could sense that many of his artifacts belonged in museums.

The afternoon of our last meeting with the Colonel, we had beers in his air-conditioned study. It was a hundred degrees outside, the humidity oppressive and debilitating—one of those days on which you could soak yourself in sweat just standing in the shade. The Colonel let us browse among his things while he told us about the need for good translators in Military Intelligence. I suppose he was trying, rather unsubtly, to recruit us with images of exotic advanced military training and skullduggery. Lew was struck with the romance of such images, but I had grown up as an Army brat, and knew the underbelly of the military life. While the Colonel told Lew about the battle of White Horse Ridge, I noticed a small stack of ricepaper pages on his desk. It was the beautiful calligraphy that caught my eye. I could only read a dozen characters, since I had only studied Classical Chinese for a few years then, but even so I could tell it was a narrative. I picked up the pages and flipped through them, thinking it odd that the Colonel would have the unbound remnants of what appeared to be an antique book. The third page was a title page, and another narrative ensued there. The title characters were *Ke* and *Niao*— "Song Bird." I interrupted the Colonel and asked him about the text. He didn't read any Chinese, he said, but if I liked the calligraphy, I was welcome to the pages. He had reams of it from an antique shop in Mary's Alley, and he used it to paper his walls. I thanked him and held up the text, which was about an inch thick. He gestured that I was welcome to it, and so I put it in my shoulder bag.

When I went back to the United States that fall, I left most of my Korean books with Lew, including the "Song Bird" text. He was far better with Classical Chinese than I, and so I told him to try his hand at reading it someday when he could make out all the archaic calligraphy. I had decided, by then, to focus on oral folklore and fiction from the modern period. I confess now that it was largely due to my laziness. I preferred to rely on my native abilities and my ear for colloquial Korean rather than pursue decades of training in the classics. Lew was more of the archival literary scholar, and so I was happy to leave him my old dictionaries and volumes of classics (which were expensive to ship back, in any case).

So that summer in Vancouver, Lew and I reminisced about our old days back in pre-Olympics Korea. After the translation work-shops—which were surprisingly fun for us—we went out for dinner, then beers, then coffee, until we wound up in his office at the University of British Columbia sometime after midnight. He wanted to show me something. A surprise after fifteen years. It took a while to rummage through the disorganized stacks of papers on his various desks, but then he found what he was looking for and handed me a dusty manila folder of A4 paper. "Have a look," he said. "Tell me if you remember what it is."

47

The pages alternated between photocopies of Classical Chinese calligraphy and English translation in which missing or unknown words were marked by blank brackets. I knew it immediately. "This is the stuff I gave you from Noakowski," I said. "You translated it."

He nodded, sitting back in his swivel chair. "Read it and tell me what you think."

"Now?" I asked. It was nearly one in the morning and we had another workshop session to attend at nine.

Lew turned on his Mac. "It's not that long," he said. "Read it and tell me if you recognize it. You're the folklorist."

I cleared a stack of dictionaries from a chair and sat down to read "Song Bird." It took only a few pages before I had an odd feeling about the story. Even with the missing parts, which Lew had attempted to paraphrase in spots, I knew what it was. It was a variant of Hans Christian Andersen's story, "The Nightingale."

The surprise on my face must have been obvious, because Lew said, "Well? I know I heard this story somewhere, but I couldn't for the life of me remember."

"It's Hans Christian Andersen," I told him. "We found a Chinese translation of 'The Nightingale.'"

"Wasn't Andersen a nineteenth century writer?"

"Yes," I said. "Most of his work was probably mid-eighteen hundreds."

Lew handed me a sheet of paper that looked like a doctor's report. I squinted at it. "I had the paper dated," he said. "The rice-paper goes back at least three hundred years."

I suggested that perhaps it was old paper which someone had finally used in the 19th Century. "The story is pretty close," I told him. "A Chinese emperor, an unearthly singer, a machine. The elements are mostly parallel from what I can see, though Andersen's is a bird and this one is a girl."

"The ink is just as old," said Lew. "Even accounting for the margin of error, the text goes back about three hundred years."

"Then this is a pretty interesting discovery," I said. I had him access one of the e-texts of Andersen's work online, and we began to compare "Song Bird" to an English translation of "The Nightingale." The parallels were uncanny, but it soon became clear that what we had was an older Asian source for Andersen's story. Lew and I spent the remainder of the night and next day, sleepless, finishing the translation and ascertaining a probable history of the Chinese text.

After a visit to the UBC Asian collection, it was clear. "Song Bird" was a 17th century Korean text contemporary to Kim Man-chung's Buddhist novel, *Nine Cloud Dream*, but it was most likely a variation of a literary form called "Strange Tales" from the middle of the Chinese T'ang Dynasty, sometime in 8th Century. (The irony, or perhaps the synchronicity, did not escape us. I had gotten the pages from a descendant of James Gale, whose translations of Classical Korean texts included one of *Nine Cloud Dream*, which he rendered as *A Cloud Dream of the Nine*.) Both my skills as a translator and my knowledge of Classical Chinese had improved since my graduate student days, and so I helped Lew put the finishing touches on his translation, working through the many blank brackets often by looking up the etymologies of the obscure characters in Korean *Ok P'yon* and in dictionaries of Chinese. I present our joint effort below.

If you do not know the Andersen story, read "Song Bird" simply as a fable written by a young 17th century Confucian scholar to entertain an old master, perhaps to earn points on the free essay component of a civil service examination. (The author's identity is yet to be discovered.) If you know "The Nightingale," you will be surprised to discover that this earlier tale has a distinctly different message. How it eventually came to Andersen and why he chose to change the story, I have yet to ascertain, but while I go back to my research, which has accumulated into quite a stack of papers in my office here in New Paltz, perhaps you will discover the answer in the story itself.

◊

Kê-Niao

for Charlotte Church

Long ago, in the mythic times before the reign of the First Emperor Chin Shi Huang Ti, there lived another emperor, a great but cruel man whose name has been forgotten. His is the tale I tell you now, before I, too, forget; because then it will be entirely lost—forever—and no one will know the truth and the mystery of the fate that befell him.

This emperor's name is not known to us, for it has been destroyed from all documents and monuments, but it is rumored that his surname was Wang, and it is from his name that we get our word for king. His palace was the most wondrous in all the world, greater than all the palaces of the past and greater, by far, than any that shall ever be. It was built of white alabaster and jade of many hues, its walls inlaid with precious and semiprecious stones. It was a place of such magnificence and delicacy that a visitor was wont to hold his breath for fear of breaking something (and the penalty for breaking anything in the Emperor's palace, as you know, was one's life, forfeited through the most hideous torture).

In the Emperor's garden one could see the rarest of flowers from the world's most exotic places, and to remind the viewer of their rarity, tiny bells of transparent gold were tied to them. And when one brushed the flowers even most gently, or even walked briskly past, the bells would tinkle melodiously, their pitches matched exactly to the color and fragrance of the blossoms from which they hung. Everything in the Emperor's garden was unique and remarkable, and it stretched so far from east to west (to match the path of the sun) that even the Imperial Gardener himself had never seen the whole of it in all his lifetime.

Those members of the Emperor's court who were fortunate enough to have traveled to the limits of his garden knew that there was a great wood, full of tall and regal trees, that extended from there down to the sandy shore that bordered the realm of the Dragon King. In this great wood—it was rumored—there lived a magical bird that sang in a human voice. So beautiful was its song that the great trading ships that sailed along the coast were often distracted and ran aground in the shallows; and their rescue was invariably delayed because the local sailors would all pause, putting off their work, to listen.

Even the fishermen, who worked day and night to feed the Emperor's court, would stop to listen; and sometimes in the evening when they sat, exhausted, to mend their nets, they would hear the song and be filled with a joy that gave them the energy to begin again the next day. "How beautiful!" they would exclaim. "How beautiful is the song of Ke-Niao!" And though they would hear the songs again and again, each time it seemed they were hearing Ke-Niao for the first time.

Envoys and ambassadors from across the world came to visit the Emperor's great city, his palace, and the gardens. But those who had come by sea and heard Ke-Niao's song declared it to be the most fabulous thing of all, and upon their return to their homes, they were full of her praise. And so it was that the scholars and historians and adventurers of distant lands wrote their weighty tomes in which they described what they knew of the Emperor's realm, and all of them singled out the song of Ke-Niao as its greatest wonder. Poets waxed sentimental and nostalgic about the ethereal song of the magical bird and memoirists all expressed, as their last wish, the hope to hear that song again.

It was only a matter of time before one of these foreign books was seen by the Emperor, for he was always suspicious and wanted to know what others thought of him. Early one morning, in his pavilion that overlooked a meander of the misty River Li, the Emperor happened upon a description of his land. It pleased him to no end to read such lavish praises heaped upon his city, his palace, and his gardens. But then he found a description of something of which he knew nothing, and he turned pale. "The magical melody of Ke-Niao, the mythic songbird known to sing in the voice of a maiden, is the most wondrous thing in the whole exotic and mysterious kingdom of Cathay," he read.

"What is this!?" shouted the Emperor. "How can there be such a thing in my empire and I not know of it?" Immediately, he flew into a rage and called together all the ministers of his High Council. And when they were gathered beneath his throne, trembling with fear, he said to them: "I have read in a foreign book that there is a magical bird in my domain. It's song is said to be the most wondrous thing in the world, and yet I have never heard of it. Why have I never been told of it? And why is it that I, of all mortal men, have never heard it?"

"I have never heard of such a bird," said the Chief Minister. "There has never been word of such a thing during all my time in your court, Your Excellency."

"It is my wish that the bird sing for me this evening," said the Emperor. "If a foreign barbarian can describe this bird and know of it more intimately than I, the Emperor, then it should be easily found."

"If such a bird exists, then I shall find it, Your Excellency."

"Indeed, you shall find it," said the Emperor. "Or you shall face my displeasure." And he dismissed his High Council.

Where was this magical bird to be found? The Chief Minister suddenly realized he was all alone, for all the others had fled at their first opportunity, not wanting to share his profound burden. The Chief Minister ran through the gleaming halls of the palace calling upon anyone who might listen to him, but the few souls he found to question had never heard of such a bird. So in his desperation he visited the Temple of Arcane Wisdom, where he sought out the High Zoomancer, and he demeaned himself by asking advice.

"Do not think me ignorant, for I am the Chief Minister chosen for my vast knowledge," he said to the Zoomancer. "But I must find what seems to be a mythic bird called a Ke-Niao. Perhaps you could tell me where one is to be found nearby?"

The Zoomancer grimaced in what appeared to be pain. "Please excuse my limited knowledge, but Ke-Niao means 'songbird,' and the name can thus refer to any of a thousand species and their many particular permutations. Perhaps if you could tell me which particular songbird you seek, most noble Chief Minister?"

"Pah!" said the Chief Minister. And now fortified with this bit of zoological knowledge, he returned to the Emperor and told him the account must be a fiction—invented, no doubt, by a foreign barbarian to add color to his description of their glorious empire. "Your Excellency," he said, "the Great Sage once said one must not believe everything one sees, and even less those things seen in the pages of books."

"The book from which I read," hissed the Emperor, "was delivered to me by one of my best spies. It was stolen from the great library of Alexandria, where all knowledge is said to abide, and therefore it cannot be a false account." He summarily dismissed the Chief Minister to endure a torture known as the Thousand Kowtows upon the Mat of Shards, and he announced to the others: "It is my intention to hear this Ke-Niao tonight. If she does not appear and sing for me, I shall have the lot of you pickled in brine at the end of the evening."

"Your Excellency," the ministers said in unison, kowtowing until their heads touched the cold, polished stone of the floor. And they dispersed to all corners of the palace, running up and down stairs from pavilion to pavilion inquiring about the mysterious bird known as Ke-Niao. Not one of them met with success, and as the day drew on the ministers began to straggle back to loiter hopelessly in the courtyard, waiting for their terrible fates.

But at last one of the ministers—an old man beyond despair— happened to ask the orphan boy who swept the courtyard.

"Oh, I have heard Ke-Niao," said the boy, too simple-minded even to speak in honorifics. "In fact, I know her quite well."

"What?" said the minister. "How is it that you can know a thing of which no one in the Emperor's court has heard?" But the other ministers had already gathered around, and they said, "Tell us! Tell us! Is this the Ke-Niao that sings with the voice of a maiden?"

The boy was afraid now, and he cast his eyes down. "Yes, she can sing, and the most wonderful songs," he said. "When I am done sweeping the courtyard at night, I return to the fishing village by the edge of the great wood. That is where I live. My father was lost at sea and my mother died of a broken heart waiting for his return."

"Enough about you!" said a young minister. "We want to hear what you know of Ke-Niao."

The boy fell to his knees in fear and mumbled apologies into the paving stones.

"Come," said the old minister, lifting him. "Tell us about Ke-Niao as you will."

"I am so tired when I return to the village. So tired and hungry, that I must stop halfway and rest by the edge of the wood. On the nights when Ke-Niao sings, I listen to her song and tears come to my eyes. . ." The boy sobbed and began to cry. ". . . because then I remember the lullabies my mother used to sing, and it is as if she is embracing me again."

"Boy," said the High Minister, "if you take us to Ke-Niao, I will post you to the imperial kitchen as a food taster, and you shall never be tired or hungry again as long as you live. Take us to her so I may invite her to sing this evening in the palace."

So the boy led the minister to the edge of the wood where Ke-Niao sang, and the others followed behind. As the procession reached the edge of the great garden, they heard a faint chanting.

"Ah," said a junior minister, "we have found her already! What wonderful singing—I have certainly heard it before."

"No, that is the chant of the Emperor's gardeners weeding," said the boy. "We have still a long way to go."

After a while, when the ministers were growing tired and complained about their shoes (which were made for the paved court, and not for walking upon a trail), they heard a faint melody.

"Beautiful," said the junior minister again. "Now I hear her.

Surely that is the voice of an enchanted maiden."

"No, that is the sound of girls singing at a village well," said the boy. "We have still farther to go."

Soon the ministers were all grumbling about the pains in their feet and the aches in their backs. Several of them removed their tight shoes and swooned at the sight of blisters on their delicate toes. Presently they heard a woman's voice resounding softly among the trees, and the junior minister leapt up, declaring, "Surely, this is she! How can a mortal man resist such enchanting music?"

"No," said the boy, "that is a woodcutter's wife singing for her husband's safe return."

By now the ministers were moaning and groaning, complaining that they could walk no farther. They began to doubt the boy's story; they sent one of their company back to fetch palanquins for their return. As they paused to rest, many of their number declaring that they could not rise again, they heard a clear melody echoing through the wood. It caused them to lift their eyes upward, to rise, to look about. In a short while even the oldest of the ministers was standing, full of energy and an unmistakable joy. The usual downward turn of their mouths had transformed into expressions of peace, and in some of them—most incredibly—into smiles. There was no doubt that what they all heard was the song of Ke-Niao.

"Look, there she is," said the boy. "There," he said, and pointed to her when the ministers looked about in confusion.

It was not a magical bird, as the ministers had expected and hoped to see. Ke-Niao was not a bird at all, but a young girl perched upon a rock in the middle of the stream, and she was washing a load of laundry as she sang.

"Can it be?" said the High Minister, "I never imagined she would be a peasant girl. Surely, she is a heavenly fairy in disguise."

"The magical bird must have taken this form to trick us," said a younger minister. "We must call the High Priest to capture her."

But it was soon clear to all that the magical voice was that of the girl. "Ke-Niao," called the boy, "the Emperor wants you to sing for him!"

"Oh, that gives me great joy," said the girl, and she began another verse that caused the ministers to listen, dumbfounded.

"More beautiful than the sound of the golden glass bells," said the High Minister, when he was again able to speak. "How is it we have never heard of her before? She will be a great success at court if we but change her homely appearance."

"Shall I sing once more for you, dear Emperor?" asked Ke-Niao. So innocent was she, that she believed herself to be in his presence.

"Sweet little girl," said the High Minister, "Do not be deceived by our regal appearance. We are to the Emperor as the stars are to the sun. I have the great pleasure of inviting you to the palace this evening, where you will gain his favor with your most excellent song."

"But if the Emperor is like the sun, then my song is best sung for him here in the wood," said Ke-Niao. But still, much to the relief of the ministers, she came willingly when she heard it was the Emperor's wish.

That evening in the palace, the walls and floors of polished alabaster and marble glowed in the light of ten thousand lamps that burned only the smokeless oil of purest pine nuts. The most exquisite flowers of the Emperor's garden, with their tiny bells of transparent gold, decorated the corridors; with all the rushing to and fro in the court, their music was so loud that one could hardly be heard to speak.

In the center of the great hall, an elegant screen had been constructed for Ke-Niao; it was made to look like a spring pavilion, and the skill of the imperial carpenters was so great that one's eye was tricked into believing it was a real pavilion in the distance, though it was only a small imitation. Ke-Niao was to sit behind this screen before a bright lantern so that her silhouette would be cast upon the paper panels. In that way could her voice be heard without its elegance being marred by her humble appearance.

All the members of the imperial court were present, all dressed in their splendid formal gowns of embroidered silk, and the orphan boy who swept the courtyard stood by the door, for he was now an apprentice to the food taster. Every eye was turned to the small pavilion in the center of the courtyard when the Emperor nodded to the Grand Master of Court Music. A command was whispered behind the screen, the silhouette moved, and an ethereal sound suddenly filled the room. It was a voice, so sweet and yet so sad that its first notes brought tears to the Emperor's eyes. Ke-Niao sang the Ballad of Longing for Home, her silhouette gesturing plaintively, and soon there was not a dry eye in the palace.

And then, when all were ready to bear their poignant melancholy, she sang another ballad that touched their hearts and filled them with a brilliant joy. The Emperor was so delighted that he forgot his initial displeasure (for he had hoped she would be a magical bird), and he declared that Ke-Niao should choose a jewel from among his personal treasures. "You may wear it around you neck to show that you have earned my favor," he said, but she declined the honor with thanks.

"I have seen the Emperor's tears," said Ke-Niao, "and that is my richest reward, for I am told they are rarer than the rarest jewels in all of Cathay." And then she sang again, more enchantingly than ever.

Indeed, Ke-Niao's visit was a most resounding success. She was now to remain at court, to have her own quarters, with liberty to go out twice during the day and once during the evening. Twelve servants were appointed to attend to her every need, and they followed her everywhere as if they were bound to her by threads of silk. There was no pleasure in this confinement, no matter how regal it appeared, for Ke-Niao was not permitted to return home; her family, being lowly peasants, were barred from the palace gates.

Everyone in the capital spoke of the wondrous Ke-Niao, and when two people met, one would say "Ke" and the other would say "Niao" and they understood what was meant, for there was no other topic of conversation. Even the children of peasants were named after her, though there was little likelihood that they would ever sing a graceful note.

Then, one day, the Emperor received a large casket on which was written, "The Songbird Mechanism."

"Here is no doubt a multi-volume account that ventures an explication of our celebrated Ke-Niao," said the Emperor. But instead of learned books, there was a work of artifice contained in the casket, a mechanical mannequin made to look like the living Ke-Niao, but covered all over with diamonds, rubies, and sapphires. Round its neck, hung a ribbon of gold foil on which was written, "From the King of Babylon, a humble gift to the Emperor of Great Cathay."

The Emperor's artificers followed the enclosed directions: they filled the accompanying jar with a solution of pungent rice vinegar, and then, waiting forty-five degrees on the intervals of the celestial clock, they uncoiled the two sheathed wires from the top of the jar and attached them to the two small spheres of gold on the mannequin's base—one yin, the other yang—being sure that the wires did not touch each other. Then they called upon the real Ke-Niao, and under the Music Master's direction, they instructed her to sing the Emperor's favorite ballad, directing her sweet voice precisely midway between the mannequin's upraised silver mesh palms.

And it was done. When the High Artificer pulled the red lever, the mannequin swayed its torso and its arms as if it were alive, and a sweet voice issued from its breast as if Ke-Niao herself were singing. But the mannequin could be made to sing most softly—at a whisper for the Emperor's sole pleasure—or it could be made to sing so loudly that the whole palace could hear without gathering in the main courtyard; all this at the turn of a metal knob or the pull of a colored lever. The mannequin's greatest advantage was that it could sing the same ballad again and again, in precisely the same way, without tiring or changing its inflection because of a mood or a vagary of thought. And furthermore, it was a remarkable work of art, beautiful to regard and admire, unlike the girl whose humble looks had to be hidden behind the paper screen. In a short while, the Emperor much preferred the mannequin.

"Marvelous!" exclaimed all who saw it. The envoy who had brought the mannequin was sent back with a caravan of gold and seven imperial engineers to advise the King of Babylon on the construction of his great tower.

"Surely, they must sing together," said the members of the imperial court, "for what a duet it would make." But they did not get on well, for Ke-Niao sang in her own way, each rendition different, though it might be the same tune, while the mannequin could only sing the same single tune again and again in exactly the same way.

"That is not a fault," said the Master of Music. "It is quite superior, for the mannequin's song endures and preserves the timelessness of a melody which the girl alters with each rendition." Of course, he did not mention the fact that the mannequin's song had been sung first by Ke-Niao. And the people did not care, for the mannequin was so much prettier to look at: it sparkled and shimmered when it moved its mechanical limbs. No one noticed that its lips did not move (or perhaps they did not point out that flaw for fear of the Emperor's displeasure).

One hundred and forty-four times did the mannequin sing the same tune without growing tired; and the people would gladly have heard it again, but the Emperor said the living Ke-Niao should sing the song as well so that all could attest to the superiority of the mannequin.

But where was Ke-Niao? No one had noticed her when she climbed out of an open window and returned to her home at the edge of the great wood.

"What uncivil conduct," the Emperor said when her flight had been discovered; and all the ministers of the court blamed her, saying she was a very ungrateful creature.

"But we have the better singer, after all," said a junior minister. "What need have we for the homely girl?" And they all listened to the song again, though it was now the one-hundred-and-forty-fifth time (and even then they had not learnt it by heart, for it was a most difficult ballad).

Now the Master of Music heaped more and higher praise upon the mechanical Ke-Niao. "You must understand, Your Excellency, that with a real singer we can never tell what is going to be sung, but with this machine everything is known before hand. And unlike a voice from the human apparatus, this one may be interrupted at any moment, thus allowing us to observe the fine transformations of tone within a single note. No human voice can match the elegance of the mechanism." And the Emperor was pleased.

"Our thoughts match those exactly," said all the minister, and then the Master of Music received permission to exhibit the mannequin to the public on the next festival day, and the Emperor commanded that they should be present to hear it sing. When they heard it they were like people intoxicated. They all praised it lavishly and kowtowed in its honor, but a poor fisherman, who had heard the real Ke-Niao, said, "It sings prettily enough, and the melodies are all alike, yet there seems something wanting. I cannot say exactly what."

And after this, Ke-Niao was found in her village and sent to the dungeons, though the Emperor spared her the usual tortures in an unexpected gesture of mercy. The miniature pavilion behind which Ke-Niao had performed was left in one corner of the Emperor's sleeping chamber, but the mannequin was placed on silk cushions and all the gifts of gold and jewels that Ke-Niao had received were arranged in decorative piles around it. Soon it was given the official title "Tai Ke-Niao Chi," which means "The Great Mechanical Songbird," and because he had decided the whole court must hear its songs each day, the Emperor had it moved to an elaborate pedestal of white jade to the left of the his throne. (That was the side from which he listened best; for common folk the left side is the side of the heart, but it is said the Emperor lacked that most human of organs.)

The Grand Master of Court Music composed a learned work about the Tai Ke-Niao Chi, which was full of the most obscure allusions to mathematics and cosmology, and yet all the court claimed to have read it and understood it for fear of annoying the Emperor. But when the Emperor himself examined the book and found it too obscure, he threw the Grand Master of Court Music into the dungeon to endure a torture called "Small Dragon Penetrates the Membrane of Sound." Though it is said to be a painless torture, all who suffer it go mad from the unbearable itching within the brain (and they are said to have the most hideous appearance afterward, from self-inflicted gouges upon their features).

So twelve months passed, and the Emperor, his court, and all of Cathay knew every minuscule turn of the mannequin's song; and now, for some reason, it did not please them quite so much. When the Emperor learned that the common folk in the streets could sing the ballad as well as he, a foul mood came over him and he ordered the public performances to stop at once. It was most disconcerting.

One evening, as the Tai Ke-Niao Chi was singing its song for the four-hundred-and-forty-fourth time and the Emperor lay in his bed listening, something went terribly amiss.

Something inside the mannequin snapped, and the beautiful voice suddenly ceased. What could be heard then was a rhythmic slapping which sounded, to the Emperor, like the whipping wheel used in the torture of Ten Thousand Lashes. The Emperor immediately sprang out of bed and called for his physician, but what could a physician do for a machine? They sent for the High Artificer who, after a great deal of mumbling and examination, made the mannequin sing again, but only through the workings of a crude hand crank. And one could hardly call the strange sounds that issued from the repaired Tai Ke-Niao Chi a song—though the tune was recognizable, the words slurred and chirped and warbled like a collection of strange birds mimicking a girl's voice.

The High Artificer explained that a vital part of the mechanism had broken from overuse, and that many other gears and wheels were worn beyond repair. The Tai Ke-Niao Chi must be used only sparingly—and very carefully—he said, if it was to work at all. He suggested that it be played only on special public occasions, and then he quickly retired to his quarters and took his own life, for he knew it was only a matter of time before the Emperor would find fault with him and order him to the dungeons.

Now there was great sorrow in Cathay, as the Tai Ke-Niao Chi was only allowed to play once a year; and even that was dangerous for the workings inside it. But the Emperor purged the court of all Masters of Music, and he declared that the mannequin's song was as good as ever. No one dared contradict him.

Four years passed, and calamities came upon the land: earthquakes, floods, famine, one after the other, until finally the ominous sign of the comet appeared. Having thus lost the Mandate of Heaven, the Emperor grew sick and now he lay so ill that he was not expected to live (and secretly, it was hoped that some bold minister would put an end to him). The people clamored for news of his death so they could celebrate, but no word yet came from the inner palace.

Cold and pale the Emperor lay in his royal bed; and the whole court waited anxiously for his death, for they were eager to appoint his successor. The ministers of the High Council conferred through a day and a night and there were many plots afoot to curry favor with the successor. Indeed, the inner palace was so busy that—under the pretext of mourning —bolts of fine cloth had been laid down in the halls and passages so that no footstep should be heard, and all was silent and still.

But the Emperor was not yet dead, though he lay stiff and pale as alabaster on his regal bed behind camphor-scented netting of the finest silk. Outside the window the full moon rose and shone its cold light upon the Emperor's feverish brow. His breath grew labored, and when at length he opened his eyes he saw that there was a silhouette on the screen of the small model pavilion. His eyes grew wide in surprise, for he thought it must be Ke-Niao, but it was not. It was the shadow of Lord Yama, ruler of the Kingdom of Death.

"I see out of respect for my position you have come in person and not sent your lowly emissaries," said the Emperor.

The Lord of Death did not answer. Instead his shadow lifted

the shadow of the Emperor's crown and put it on.

"I will not go so easily," hissed the Emperor.

The Lord of Death raised his arms, and now, slowly intermingled with the moonbeams, shade after shade appeared, the ghosts of all the innocents the Emperor had tortured and executed. They all bore the expressions they had worn at the time of their death, and many were hideous or pathetic or pitiful to behold. A few faces were tranquil, and these scared the Emperor far more than the others.

"Do you remember us?" they asked, one after the other. "Do you remember what you did to us?" they whispered in their plaintive voices.

The Emperor clamped his eyes shut and turned his face away from them. "I remember none of you!" he cried bitterly. "Music! Music! Clang the gongs! Ring the bronze bells! Anything to drown out these voices!" But the ghosts went on and on and the shadow of Lord Yama nodded to them from behind the screen.

"Sing!" the Emperor cried to the mannequin. "Sing, you infernal machine! I've showered you with gold and jewels that would be the envy of princes. I've thrown mortals whimpering into my dungeons for you! Sing for me!"

But the mannequin was silent and still, for the foreign magic that gave it life had finally run out and no one knew how to restore it.

The Lord of Death continued to regard the Emperor with his fiery eyes, which flickered in the shadow of his face, and the room was fearfully still. Suddenly there came through the open window the sound of an ethereal voice.

It was Ke-Niao, outside in the cool moonlight, singing the seven-part ballad of Virtue and Longing. And as she sang, the ghosts grew paler and paler; the blood flowed more freely in the Emperor's veins, returning life to his limbs. Even Lord Yama himself listened, distracted from his task, showing his pleasure with nods of his shadowy head.

At the end of the first verse, the Emperor turned his head toward her and said, "Ke-Niao, dear Ke-Niao, do not stop now.

Please, sing the next verse."

"What have you to give me then?" she replied.

"I am on my deathbed, little girl, and my life is dearer to me than anything. I give you my imperial crown."

So Ke-Niao sang the next verse, and the Emperor and the Lord of Death listened, and when it was done the Emperor said, "Ke-Niao, dear Ke-Niao, please do not stop now. Please, sing the next verse."

"What have you to give me then?" she replied.

"I am on my deathbed, little girl, and my life is dearer to me than anything. I give you my imperial seal."

And so Ke-Niao sang the next verse, and the next, and the next, and each time the Emperor gave up more of his worldly possessions. By the end of the sixth verse, he had relinquished all the territories of his vast empire, his golden sword and his grand armies, the fantastic treasures in his coffers, his ownership of ten million slaves.

As she concluded the sixth verse, the Emperor said, "Ke-Niao, dear Ke-Niao, you cannot stop now. Please, sing the final verse."

"And what have you to give me?" asked Ke-Niao.

The Emperor was quiet for a while, and then he said, "I am on my deathbed, little girl, and my life is dearer to me than anything." And then, in a whisper, he said, "I have nothing left to give you, dear Songbird."

Ke-Niao bowed her head in apology. "I am sorry, my dear Emperor," she said, "but if you have nothing left to give, then I cannot sing the final verse."

The Emperor closed his eyes and was still. His breaths grew shallow, and under his eyelids his eyes moved as if they would roll upward in death. All was quite for the longest time, and then it was the Lord of Death who broke the silence.

"Sing," he said, in his sonorous voice. "You cannot stop after six verses."

"And what have you to give me, Lord Yama?" asked Ke-Niao. "What can you give me that the great Emperor could not give?"

"I give you his life," said the Lord of Death, and there was a rumble in his throat, and his silhouette seemed to grow and engulf the room before it receded once again to be contained by the screen.

"Thank you, my lord," said Ke-Niao, and she sang the seventh and final verse of the song. She sang of the silent tumuli where the ancients are buried, where white peonies grow among the dolmens of stone, where the mimosa trees waft their perfume on the breeze and the sweet grass is wet with dew of morning.

Then the Lord of Death longed to go and see such beauty, and he floated out through the open window in the form of a cold, white mist.

"Thank you, thank you," said the Emperor. "Ten thousand thank-yous, little Ke-Niao. I replaced you with a mannequin and caste you into my dungeon, and yet you have returned with your song. And though I failed your test, still you saved me from death. How can I ever reward you, Ke-Niao, for I wish to give you something more, and you have left me nothing but my life."

"You have already rewarded me more than you know," said Ke-Niao. "You wept the first time I sang for you, and I shall never forget that, for those tears were more precious than all the great riches you gave up tonight. I could not let Lord Yama take you, dear Emperor, for how could I let you die when you have never truly lived? Now sleep and grow well again, so you may learn why life is more precious than anything."

And as she sang again, the Emperor fell into a deep, healing sleep.

When he awoke, his fever had broken and the last beams of the setting moon shone through his window. He sat up, feeling his ch'i, his life force, restored, and he pulled down the camphored curtains and cast them across the floor. No servant had ventured into his room during the night. Only Ke-Niao was there, sitting at his bedside, barely visible; she seemed as insubstantial as the moonlight, and yet she was still softly singing.

"You must stay with me always," said the Emperor, gently. "You may sing when it pleases you, and the tunes may be of your own choosing. I will destroy this infernal machine."

"No," said Ke-Niao. "Do not destroy the machine, for it did merely what was its nature. Keep it as a reminder. I cannot remain here, and I cannot linger in my village, but let me come and sing for you from time to time."

The Emperor smiled, but his eyes remained sad.

"Do not worry, dear Emperor," said Ke-Niao. "I return to you everything you have given me, for in giving you have reclaimed all that is yours. I will sing to you from a bough outside your window, in the evening, and sing to you so that you may be happy. I will sing to you of joys and sorrows, of those who prosper and those who suffer, of the good and the bad that are all around you. Wherever you are, I will come, and I will sing to you. But you must promise me one thing."

In the last light of the moon, she was paler than the most regal courtesan. For an instant the Emperor marveled at how a homely peasant girl had become such a beauty, and then he knew that neither her pallor nor her beauty were of this world, for she was no longer flesh, but made of the waning light.

"Anything," said the Emperor, and his voice cracked and tears filled his eyes. "I promise you anything, Ke-Niao—even my life, for now that is rightfully yours and not mine."

"I ask only that when I come to sing for you again, I will sing to a man and not an Emperor." And with these words, Ke-Niao bowed and took her leave. When the mist cleared from the Emperor's eyes and he could see again, the moon had set and she was gone.

It is said that when the servants came in the morning to tend to him, they found the Emperor's bed empty. The court was in an uproar, but only briefly, because everyone had hated the man. No funeral was held, for there was no body. And when the successor took the imperial throne, things went on as if the old Emperor had never ruled. Indeed, he was so reviled that all mention of his name was stricken from the official histories.

It is also said—and this may be mere legend—that the Emperor had left in the night, changing into humble clothes and washing the dye from his hair. No one recognized the wizened old man who limped out of the gates of the great city and wandered into the mountains to become a hermit. They say that having lived his first life as Emperor, Wang lived his next as a mere man, and so he finally learned what it was, truly, to live as a mortal should.

◊

光

What is the use of talking,
        and there is no end of talking,
There is no end of things in the heart.

—Li Po (701-762)
"Exile's Letter"

Gone

No rustle of silk—
      dust drifts over the courtyard;
No sound of footfalls—
      the mounds of crackling leaves, now still.

And she is there, beneath them,
      love of my heart,
A wet leaf
      clinging at the gate.

—Han Wu Ti (156-87 B.C.)

羽

And I, wrapped in brocade,
      went to sleep with my head on his lap,
And my spirit so high it was all over the heavens.

          —Li Po (701-762)
           "Exile's Letter"

In the Garden of Lumbini
(from *Siddhartha Gautama*)

I.

That night was the end of the festival, and now the streets were quiet once again. The last jingle of ankle bells had died down into the silence of the night, still radiant with moonlight. Seven days, and now the seventh night, and Queen Maya lay asleep, wrapped in fragrance and dream, her lord, the Raja beside her, breathing the calm breath of a man at ease. That day, fresh-scented from her morning bath, the Queen had robed herself in bright but muted colors; she had ventured out into the city where the people sang joyously, where the women raised their bangled arms to strew flowers into the air and the sunlight and shadow mingled among the luminous falling petals. It was the mid-summer Festival of the Full Moon.

To her sister, Prajapati, the Queen had smiled a wan smile tinged with longing, and she had said, "Oh, Prajapati, I am forty-five. Near half a century gone and I have yet to bear a child. If only I could share this happiness, if only I could be full like the moon we honor, and give my lord a son." And Prajapati had said, "I know, in my heart, that the gods favor you, sister, and you will be fruitful." And Maya, comforted, gave alms to the poor that day — forty thousand pieces of gold that caught the light of the sun and flickered like miniature lamps leaping from hand to brown hand — as people thronged the streets of Kapilavastu praising the name of Queen Maya and her lord, Suddhodana Gautama of the Shakya clan.

And now they lay asleep. The heat had waned. The seventh

day of the Full Moon Festival, the seventh night, bathed in silver and touched by the breath of the gods. Maya dreamed.

She, whose name means illusion, lay in her bed at her husband's side looking up at the darkness, and yet it was not darkness. She could see through the high canopy of the bed, up through the ceiling of the bedchamber—there, the carved white alabaster of the moon, still nearly full, looked like the belly of a woman in silhouette. And in the heavens, near it, sparkled a star, rotating its golden light until six distinct beams shone down, six rays twirling, growing larger and larger; and she felt her bed being lifted. She was no longer with the Raja but alone up in the high mountains, and yet in the rarified air she was not cold. A light bathed her, silver and gold; and in its radiance she knew great comfort.

As she lay there wondering how her lord and husband had vanished, four luminous figures appeared, one for each of the cardinal points. She could not make out their features—their faces were masked in light. They were the gods of the four quarters, and as she realized this and gasped in surprise and fear, the bed rose, spinning, beneath her. She rose into the air, through the transparent ceiling, into the night sky. She ascended and flew northward to the very tops of the great Himalayan peaks, which are the abode of the gods.

She wanted to speak to those figures of light—one at each corner of the bed—but they were silent, and in her fear she clamped down her teeth and simply watched as the world receded below her. Even in the darkness she could see. The fields and paths became a patchwork of greens and browns stitched with dark seams and the blue threads of water. Clouds turned to mist as the bed rose through them; they sealed them-selves again beneath her, until what she saw below was a single solid surface of cotton batting that went on and on, farther than her eye could follow. Her hair grew disheveled and flew behind her as she knelt on the bed and squinted to see what lay ahead. She blinked her watering eyes, saw the snow-topped crags approach, and then they were through, and what lay below was a lake—pristine blue like the eyes of an infant. In the cold air that did not chill her, the gods lowered the bed until it rested on the lake's shore; and in that unearthly quiet, she heard the water lapping against the legs of the bed.

Now the four figures disappeared—or, rather, they chang-ed radiance, from gold to silver—and Maya knew that who stood before her were the goddesses, the wives of the ones who had brought her. She was no longer afraid, but filled with joy and awe. She began to ask something, but one of the goddesses raised a finger, as if to chastise her, and she remained silent.

There was music now. A low hum that rose in pitch until it resonated—a single perfect note—from everywhere at once. The goddesses took her by the hand and led her from the bed until she stood with her feet in the shallow water. It surprised her—so clear she could not even see it. She knew it was there from the cool wetness.

The goddesses removed her clothes. At first she tried to cover her nakedness, but then they led her by the hands, into the water. They bathed her, anointing her with rare perfumes, washing her body with gentle touches of their silver fingers until the sensation made her shiver, as if from cold, though she was pleasantly warm. The sweet and minty fragrance of the perfume, the refreshing air like the breeze from a waterfall, the sound of the single cosmic note—she became sleepy, and a voice—sounding so close she turned her head to see—said, "They have purified you and now you are worthy to behold me."

She turned her head the other way. There, on the silvery peak of a mountain, stood a magnificent creature, so white its form was nearly lost in its blinding light. The star was gone and the moon was gone, and what stood before her was a bull elephant, pale and regal, greater than any elephant she had ever seen—greater than one could have seemed even in the eyes of a child. He raised his trunk as if to greet her, like a monarch acknowledging her presence; he raised his trunk, serpentine like the coil of a white Naga, and he turned that trunk and she watched, for she could not take her eyes from it. The tip of it seemed to mouth words at her. It was pink and sensitive as human lips, and she tried to hear. It was whispering, but as she drew her ear close—for now she was no longer on the bed—what came was not a sound but a beautiful lotus blossom, bursting open. It appeared so suddenly it scared her and she drew back. And now the elephant reared up, curving its trunk up high, suddenly revealing its six tusks of purest ivory, and he began to run, once, twice, three times around her coiled form, and when she looked—out of the corner of her eye, for she was afraid—deathly afraid, and yet deathly calm, unearthly calm—the elephant whipped its trunk at her right side. She felt the rush of air and she feared the power of the blow to come; but the blow did not come. Instead, she felt something burst within her as if a seed had exploded, as if a bud had suddenly sprouted a flower. She could hear it pop in her ears and yet she knew it was in her womb, and then suddenly all the lights were there again and with them the sun-like radiance that outshone the white snows of the Himalayas. She saw it behind her closed eyes; she could hear it—a single wondrous note sung in tribute to her, and as she opened her eyes to see her husband sleeping at her side, she knew without a doubt, with certainty—with absolute dream certainty—that she was with child.

2.

Three seasons passed. It was spring, the month of Vaisakha, and the moon was growing full. When it came time for Maya to bear her child, she asked her lord if she could begin the trip to her natal home, as was the custom. Devadaha was not far— only two days to the east and northward. The Raja, though still concerned about her dream, gave assent, and preparations were made in the palace. There were horses and pack animals whose trappings were to be decorated—horns to wrap in colored streamers, flanks to paint in celebratory shades, manes to be braided and adorned with light-catching jewels and beads. The Raja would spare no trouble or cost to make his wife's journey both magnificent and comfortable. His advisors hand-picked the ladies in waiting and the servant girls; the bearers were the strongest in the land; the warrior guards proven in victorious battles.

And there was another thing—a troubling thing—that Suddhodana attended to: the power of signs and portends to affect Maya's delicate temperament, for she was prone to visions and dreams, too easily swayed by the words of rishis and soothsayers. Many a dream interpreter Suddhodana had expelled from the palace or had his lieutenants quietly dispatch, planting appropriate rumors of their sudden or unannounced departure for points unknown.

Maya still dwelt upon her dream. It haunted her, for the interpreters had been of many minds, and each time she noticed the snowy peaks to the north, she would recall the silver mountain and the golden light, troubling herself to know meanings that should not be known to any mortal.

Seven days before the full moon, the Raja called his advisors to him and explained the problem. They listened. They pondered. They made their learned recommendations, cast the Queen's horoscope to determine the most auspice course of action, provided wisdom from the vedas that might comfort or confound her; and to each response, Suddhodana said, "No." Indeed, there was only one solution if Maya's thoughts were troubled by the sight of the Himalayas.

"She must not see the mountains again until after she has delivered my son," he declared. "Her mind cannot be vexed so close to his arrival. The signs have all said he is to be a king of kings, and I shall not have his character made weak by his mother's anxious thoughts."

"O, Maha-Raja," they said, "The Himalayas are great, and we are but small men. Keep the Queen indoors and your purpose is achieved."

"She is no animal to be caged," said Suddhodana. "I shall not have her pleasure of movement impeded. Speak to me wisely, or you shall displease me."

"O, Maha-Raja, if the Queen must not see the mountains and

the mountains can neither be moved nor hid, then it only follows that the Queen be moved or hid," said one advisor.

"Or, O Maha-Raja, certain objects may be placed between the Queen's eyes and that which she must not behold. Things pleasing to the eye may achieve this—colorful and decorative screens, the overlapping of fans, blinds of flowers or peacock feathers. Many things may achieve the purpose."

"Good," said Suddhodana, "let this be done. And let it be done in such a way that all of these obstructions seem not products of artifice, but of natural circumstance."

"Yes, O Maha-Raja."

"And let the diversions continue until my son has breathed the sweet air of this world."

"Yes, O Maha-Raja. . . . But—"

Suddhodana's eyes flashed at this word. He looked at the brahmin who had dared to bring up this suggestion of a complication. "But?"

"But—O, Maha-Raja—the Queen will be traveling outside the palace, on the road to her father's house. Are we to place such diversions and obstructions along the entire path?"

"I leave the particulars to you, since you are wise men. And I trust in your success, or you shall know my displeasure." And so Suddhodana dismissed them, and they scattered to their meeting rooms and courtyards and gardens to make real the illusion.

The advisors called together all the magicians, the engineers, the geometers, the dramatists, and the artificers—all those who worked upon appearances that confounded the real and the seeming. They might have called upon shramanas and rishis rumored to control the minds of others, or those said to work their power over reality and dream; but Surya's word of caution had spread quickly among the brahmins, and no such assistance came forth.

3.

And finally, a great deception was organized. It was to be a grand theatrical production, in constant motion, performed all hours of the day and night. The Raja forbade the use of potions, which the herbalists said would make the distances appear but a blur to the Queen. He denounced the shramanas who said they could sooth her thoughts to give her comfort. For how was he to know—he said—that the effect of the drugs would wane and his wife regain her sharp-sightedness; how to know that some ascetic, calming her mind, would not leave there thoughts to make her renounce this material world and become a mendicant herself?

Along the road from Kapilavastu to Devadaha, a two days' walk, runners surveyed the northern aspect. Wherever there appeared a gap in the northward forest, where a tributary road or path branched from the main trunk, wherever a clearing broke the green veil of the foliage, the royal gardeners planted lush new trees, tall and thick with leaves of dark green, and these would hide the blue-white silhouette of the Himalayas. Where the rocky earth proved too hard to dig, they placed hedges of tall bamboo in massive pots. And according to the geometers—and this con-firmed by archers, to whom such concerns mean life and death—if the Queen's palanquin kept close to the northern screen, she would not see the mountains even if she emerged to enjoy the forest or stretch her limbs.

On those occasions, her attendants, who had rehearsed their motions like a dance, would draw close and fan her with peacock feathers or clear the air with specially-constructed whisks to ob-struct her view even further. And so, when the time came, a troop of engineers waited in the forest along the northern side of the road with pots of wet wood soaked in the essence of plant oils—mint, jasmine, anise—to burn when the procession drew near; and this would provide the final assurance, in the form of a pale smoke, appearing like natural mist to keep Maya's eyes from beholding the peaks.

On the day before the full moon, the procession left for

Devadaha. The Raja said his good-byes to his wives, neither of whom knew of the grand charade, and he watched from the gates of the city as they set out, teary-eyed, for they would miss him. He marveled at the frailty of their emotions—even Prajapati, who had already borne him a daughter.

"This we shall never know," he said to his chief advisor. "How a spirit in the belly moves us to be so delicate—like a plume of incense smoke in windless a room."

"It is a divine mystery, O Maha-Raja."

"And this is also a mystery," he said. "Until now I have conducted myself as if I knew with absolute certainty that Maya will bear me a son. But I am terribly afraid, Gandiva. What if it is a girl? The doubt has nagged at me from the first day."

"All the dream readers and astrologers have assured you, O Maha-Raja. How can you doubt their combined wisdom?"

"Talk to me as a man and a friend, Gandiva. I have heard enough talk from my sycophants to last me this lifetime."

"Yes . . . As you please, my lord."

"I am a kshatriya, and my station is that of a warrior, but I am not an ignorant man. I make my sacrifices to the spirits of my ancestors, and I desire a son who will sacrifice to me when I am dead. That I know. And I know that the priests and astrologers and dream readers and rishis can be wrong as much as they are right. They do not know—any more than I—what my child will be."

"But they all agree this time, my lord. That is rare."

"It is because they all know as well as any plowman or serving girl in my kingdom that what I desire and what I need is a son."

"May I ask a terrible thing?"

"Ask me, Gandiva. What could be more terrible than this uncertainty? I have waited twenty years. My ministers, including you, have entreated me to have a son by another wife, and I have foolishly refused for my love of Maya. What could be more terrible?"

"What if the child is a girl?"

The Raja regarded his wrists, jeweled with semiprecious

stones. "What is so terrible about that? Then I will have two daughters and things will go on as they have. I will grow older. Perhaps I will relent and listen to your rational advice."

"I was afraid, my lord, that with your hopes raised so high you might do something rash."

"If I wanted to purge my ministers or behead a few astrologers, what real difference would that make? I am a sober king and I know my duty to my people is to maintain my power against my rival kingdoms like Maghada."

"I have seen you disappointed before."

"I am older and wiser now, Gandiva. Should I become foolish, let me vent my anger in a safe way. And should I weep, be sure I do it not before my women or my ministers."

Gandiva bowed his head. "I know your heart is full of hope, my lord. And I tell you this—I too know that the dream readers and astrologers merely change their tales when they are wrong. They turn the blame upon the ones who consult them. So consider—if they are wrong about your child-to-be, who will they blame? There is great risk for them, for if they cast the blame upon you, they are likely to endanger their own welfare. And that is why I believe them this time. They—all of them—have taken on great risk."

"Oh, Gandiva, you merely show me how much your own heart has also been touched by this. If they are wrong, they will not dare to blame me or Maya. They will find a way to look past us and blame the stars. Or perhaps they will blame a sorcerer from another land or even dare to blame the gods."

"You are wise, Suddhodana."

"Come, let us go enjoy some distraction in the pavilion. There is a new dancing girl I would like you to see." The Raja clapped his hands, and his anxious attendants came running. They fanned away the sheen of sweat that had covered him as he stood in the sun. They put cool drinks within his reach, and he handed a gilded cup to his minister. "Tell me, Gandiva, what do you really think of Maya's dream?"

Gandiva regarded the cup as if it contained poison, but he

answered, "I do not believe it. I do not believe it was a dream."

And Suddhodana smiled an uneasy smile.

4.

No dust clouded the road to Devadaha, for water bearers had placed cisterns at intervals and runners had prepared the way by spreading water—just enough to dampen the dust, but not so much as to make the earth muddy. Leading the procession was a white bull elephant bedecked in jeweled harnesses and gilded fabrics to symbolize the auspicious dream and the glory of the Shakyas; but beneath its decorations it also wore armor to show the power of the Shakyas and to warn away the spies of neighboring lands. Inside the armored howdah mounted on the elephant's back rode keen-eyed archers who, from their high vantage, scouted ahead along the green plain, their eyes scanning the horizon, looking into stands of forest, vigilant for the slightest sign of something amiss. At intervals they signaled with bright banners to announce that all was well.

For leagues it stretched, this procession grander than any caravan, with camels and horses and donkeys all adorned in scarlet, saffron, silver, and gold, flashing with jewels and semi-precious stones, swaying with rainbow-feathered headdresses. The Raja knew the value of such glory, but he knew also the risk of such endeavor, and so he had made it as much a military campaign as a customary journey for the mother of his son-to-be. To the north and south, unseen by the Queen or her sister, Suddhodana's elite warriors secretly followed through the forest. No possibility had been overlooked.

The procession of eight thousand moved slowly, oxen and horses taking deliberate steps. To mask the sound of creaking harnesses and clanking metal, musicians played soothing melodies around Queen Maya's palanquin. Prajapati rode with her to keep her company, to talk with her of pleasant things, to attend to the slightest sign of pain or distress—but there was none. Midwives and physicians, herbalists and chakra healers, they walked or rode, according to their station, near the Queen. Serving girls and ladies in waiting—as many as a thousand—all walked nearby, and to the front and rear of the procession marched the best of the soldiery wearing ceremonial armor, their weapons polished and gleaming in the sun.

"Oh, Prajapati, already I grow weary," said the Queen. "How will I endure this journey when I am so anxious that each league seems a thousand?"

"The brahmins say that time grows longer and shorter according to the speed of our thoughts. Slow your thoughts, sister, and time will seem to fly."

"It is all seeming, so they say." A lady-in-waiting fanned her, another adjusted the orange gauze curtain; Maya pulled aside her sari and the servants averted their eyes. "I am ready to burst. How he kicks and pushes in there, to be let out, but he has been quiet today." She lay back, on her right side, placing a hand gently on her round belly, as if to touch the child inside.

"Do not worry, Maya. All I have told you is true, but you have only to trust in the gods, for they have guided you each step of this path."

"I fear the pain. It comes so suddenly, and though I know it will come, I do not know when, and each time it strikes by surprise, like an assassin."

Prajapati waved her hand as if to shoo away the inauspicious words. "Oh, that is Suddhodana and not you speaking! An assassin! No wonder you are so anxious. Perish such thoughts and think of the son you are to bear. There is great happiness in your belly."

As the morning drew to an end, as shadows grew short and the heat grew thick, Maya looked out of her palanquin, moving the curtains aside. To the north she saw a late mist lingering above the trees, which were especially lush this year. "Prajapati, do you smell it?"

"Smell what, sister?"

"I smell *sal* blossoms. We must be near Lumbini, Prajapati. Let us stop in the garden there. It is so unearthly hot in this box."

Prajapati clapped her hands and an attending minister drew close to the curtains. "We will stop at Lumbini," she said.

"Lumbini? It will take hours to make preparations, Maharini. The Maha-Raja said we were to reach Devadaha as soon as possible."

"The noon hour approaches, and we will be stopping to rest. Let us do it at the grove in Lumbini."

5.

There, between the gauzy screens—light enough to let through the breeze—they walked, hidden from the eyes of the entourage. The orange-and-yellow walls of fabric led down the gentle slope to the water, and Maya said, "I want to bathe, Prajapati. Wait for me here." She left her sister at the water's edge; she drew off her necklaces, raising them with her long, bangled arms. Metal chimed against metal. She unwrapped her sari, closing her eyes against the confusion of patterns; she dropped her veil; she stepped lightly over the green grass and descended into the pool.

She could hear the somnolent hum of bees, the cooing of doves, the warbling of other birds hidden in the grove. In the cool water she looked up into the branches of the sal trees, full of clustered orange flowers, and she thought of the child in her womb, floating, as she was floating now. She felt no weight, as if she too were suspended in a bubble of water—the child within her, she within the pool like the womb of her own mother.

When she felt refreshed, she waded out, feeling the water slide from her brown skin. She stood naked at the edge of the pool, holding one hand below her belly as the weight grew suddenly heavy and the water trickled from her, a rivulet down her thighs, not cool, but hot. She walked upward into the shade beneath the sal trees. She smelled the sudden intensity of the flowers, which fell now in a rain around her. "Prajapati!" she called, "The water—the water is so hot!"

Her sister ran to her and, hearing the commotion, the ...
wives and ladies-in-waitng came from around the screen bearing a
couch and cushions for the Queen to lie on. But Maya walked to
the *sal* tree and reached out to steady herself against a branch that
had swayed downward in the breeze. She rested her right arm
against it and called out—she did not know if it was in pain—the
sound echoed in her ear. She took firm hold of the branch, her eyes
on the clusters of bright orange-red flowers, and calling out again,
she bore down until she felt as if she would burst and the whole
world with her. She heard Prajaptai's voice speaking something to
her, the midwives crouched at her feet babbling, and she bore
down again, pushing and pushing until her vision grew dim and
the great pressure was suddenly gone. "A son!" cried a voice. "A
son!" But Maya could only hear it vaguely. She was looking at the
gauzy screens swaying gently in the wind, shimmering like
colored water; she saw clouds roiling above, flashes of divine
lightning in the distance; she heard a thunderous voice, like a
lion's roar, and it said, "I have come. I have come to bring the
Dharma to this world, to end all suffering, and this shall be my last
incarnation." Maya looked down and saw her infant boy rise up
and take seven steps northward, and in each of his footprints
blossomed a lotus of purest white. He was beautiful, golden-
skinned. She closed her eyes, her head tilted back, and saw the
sun. She opened her eyes. "Oh, Maya, you are blessed," came
Prajapati's voice. "He came without crying. He cooed like a dove,
and not a mark of hardship on him. See how he shines like a
jewel?" Maya smiled and said something to her son, held aloft in
Prajapati's arms, but she could not hear her own voice for the
thunderous cheering, the loud murmur—like the sound of break-
ing waves—and it spread among the eight thousand attendants
until it receded like a distant rain.

◊

Crossing Ching-men
to See a Friend Off

Crossing far Ching-men, and beyond,
We travel through the land of Ch'u.
Mountains fall into the wide plain;
Rivers rush to vast wilderness;
The moon flies low, like a mirror in the sky;
Clouds birth terraced tangles above the sea.
Still, you so love the waters of your native town,
I've come ten thousand *li* to see your boat depart.

—Li Po (701-762)

Afterword

The cover of Pound's *Cathay* is somewhat misleading when one thinks about it. The Chinese character on the upper left is balanced by the word "Cathay" in the lower right—and that is all, except for the name, "Ezra Pound," just underneath. Those who do not know Chinese are likely to assume that the cover says "Cathay" in two languages.

But the Chinese logograph has nothing to do with Cathay. It is read YÜEH: "glorious" or "glory." It can also be read as YAO (though that is written with the fire radical, HUO, on the left, and not KUANG), in which case it would be glossed as "illumine" or "bright," making it closer to Fenollosa's reading: "rays."

The word "Cathay" itself is a medieval European term for China derived from Marco Polo's use of "Catai" to designate northern China. The word comes from "Khitan" or "Kitai," which was the Chinese name of a northern non-Han tribe.

Given Pound's penchant for wordplay, perhaps he intended the title *Cathay* to serve as an associative connection between the archaic use of "Cathay" (as a reference to China) and the European association of "Cath" with the Greek *katharoi*, meaning "pure ones" (the Cathars, who derived their name from the same Greek word, were considered heretics by the Inquisition). The "rays" of the Chinese logograph would be a pure light, a "cathar ray." Fenollosa had glossed it in his essay as the light of the moon, the reflected light of the sun.

But I think something else was going on. The component graphs of YÜEH are:

羽 YÜ: wings, plumes;

隹 CHIA: beautiful & good;

光 KUANG: light, glory, naked, only, to adorn.

Pound was ever the egotist. At that time in his life, he was the world's pre-eminent English-language imagist, deconstructing Chinese logographs, which he believed, via Fenollosa, were ideograms full of picture-language. I think Pound designed the cover of *Cathay* as a kind of talisman. The graph for "wings," for him, designated the feathers of his symbolic quill pens. They are poised above what they write on the page: goodness and beauty, which characterize his poetry. That poetry is "naked," singular, and full of "glory," constituting "light"; the whole endeavor is "glorious." The cover of *Cathay* is Pound signifying himself as the brilliant heretic of poetry out to illuminate the world. He would have wanted to achieve no less back in those days before his public anti-Semitism cast a pall over his career, before he was incarcerated as a fascist-collaborator and then institutionalized as a madman. And yet, to some degree, I think that Pound's self-praise was well-deserved—in my reckoning, *Cathay*, despite all its problems, is his finest work.

I studied Classical Chinese for a while in the early 1980s during my graduate student days at the University of California in Davis. Those were happy times for me as a writer, since I had just begun to study folklore and translation in an academic context. While I took my fiction writing workshops with Diane Johnson, I went beyond the English department to pursue independent study courses with Marian Ury, who translated old Japanese folktales, and Ben Wallacker, who worked on ancient Chinese law and had studied Classical Chinese at Berkeley with the now mythic Peter Boodberg. Under Ben Wallacker's tutelage, I learned Classical Chinese via the unorthodox Boodberg method mediated by long sessions of guided readings in texts like the *Tao Te Ching* and *Chuang Tzu*. But it was the T'ang poetry that I found especially challenging and rewarding—even when I had to look up every single word of a long poem.

The nature of Classical Chinese forces a beginner to translate and interpret quite consciously and willfully at first. Even in a four-line poem of five-character lines, it is difficult to keep all the words in memory without writing them down, and so to read is to do textual translation. One naturally ends up with a Fenollosa-esque crib of the poems one wants to read. That is how I came to do my own translations, some of them with the assistance of Wai Lim Yip's glosses in *Chinese Poetry: An Anthology of Major Modes and Genres*. It was later, in comparing Yip to Fenollosa and my translations to those in *Cathay*, that I was able to deduce Pound's methodology. What I learned from him has served me well both in my translations of Classical Chinese and Korean works and in my own writing.

One of Pound's aspirations as a translator, I think, was eventually to do justice to the works of Wang Wei, whom he knew in Fenollosa's notebooks as Omakitsu. The translations of Li Po (Rihaku) that appear in his *Cathay* might only have been warm-ups performed on the works of a more accessible poet. Pound, for numerous and complex reasons—not all having to do with poetry—parted ways with the label of imagism not long after the publication of *Cathay*, and his attempts at translating Wang Wei, whom he called, in a 1916 letter, the "eighth century Jules Laforgue Chinois," appear mostly hidden among his Cantos. He seems to have been unsatisfied by the short translation he published in *The Little Review* in 1918. In *Cathay* itself, Wang Wei appears only in the epigraph to "Four Poems of Departure," and even then with the attribution: "Rihaku or Omakittsu." That is an unfortunate loss for the world of poetry, and I often wonder what Pound would have done if he had pursued Wang Wei at length in a sequel to *Cathay*.

◊

The short story called "Song Bird" is my response to Hans Christian Andersen's "The Nightingale," his tribute to the famous soprano, Jenny Lind (who was known as "The Swedish Nightingale"). For Andersen, the Chinese setting was probably just an exotic backdrop, but I found the orientalist misrepresentations problematic and set out to reimagine the story from a seemingly authentic T'ang Dynasty perspective. Much of my text directly incorporates the 1872 translation of "The Nightingale" by H.P. Paull. The central scene in "How Master Madman Came to Ch'ing Feng Temple" comes from a Buddhist teaching tale, and I have built the emulation of the T'ang Dynasty genre of "strange tale" (*chuanji*) around it. "The Reincarnation of Hsieng-chen" is my translation of the opening chapter of Kim Man-jung's 17th century Buddhist novel, *Nine Cloud Dream*, which some Korean scholars maintain (despite conflicting evidence) is the oldest major narrative text written in the Korean alphabet, *Han'gul*. Finally, "In the Garden of Lumbini" is the opening of *Siddhartha Gautama,* my fictional rendition of the life of the Shakyamuni Buddha up to his enlightenment under the *palsa* tree. The sources for that text include the *Pali Canon,* the *Lalitavistara,* the *Buddhacarita,* and some early Chinese texts in translation. I have also incorporated several phrases from the 1891 Roberts Brothers edition of Sir Edwin Arnold's blank verse epic, "The Light of Asia; or, The Great Renunciation." I stand on the shoulders of many giants, and sometimes I wonder if it is by karmic happenstance that I am translating *Nine Cloud Dream* and finishing my own novel about the Buddha's life at the same time.

◊

Chiang-nan

Everyone praises the beauty of Chiang-nan,
Where I shall end my wandering days—
On the spring water, bluer than the sky,
Asleep, on a painted boat, in the rain.

A woman—pale as the moon—serves me wine,
Her wrists bright frost and frozen snow.
I am not old yet—I cannot go back home.
Returning home would surely break my heart.

—Wei Chuang (836?-910)

Acknowledgments

Many thanks to David Appelbaum for his encouragement and enthusiasm as I compiled this collection, which might otherwise never have been; to Bella, the 9-year-old master of design; and to Anne, who introduced me to Pound in the first place via her interest in H.D. ("The old enchantment holds.") Thanks also to the Korean Literature Translation Institute for their generous support for my new translation of Kim Man-jung's *Nine Cloud Dream*, and to John Einarsen of *The Kyoto Journal*, for allowing us to use the sublime cover illustration. Thanks to Kirsten Snipp, for her suggestions on the first draft of "Master Madman," and special thanks to Ron Patkus for his thoughtful arguments, both aesthetic and pragmatic, for why the title of this book had to be *Cathay* and not *Kathay*.

About the Author

Heinz Insu Fenkl is an internationally renowned author, editor, translator, and folklorist. His first book, *Memories of My Ghost Brother*, an autobiographical novel about growing up in Korea as a bi-racial child in the '60s, was a Barnes and Noble "Discover Great New Writers" book in 1996 and a finalist for the PEN/Hemingway Award for First Fiction in 1997. He is also co-editor of two major collections of Korean American fiction: *Kŏri* and *Century of the Tiger*. He is currently the recipient of a fellowship from the Korean Literature Translation Institute to translate the 17th century Korean Buddhist masterpiece, *Nine Cloud Dream*. Fenkl was raised in Korea, Germany, and the United States. He lives in the Hudson Valley with his wife and daughter and teaches at the State University of New York, New Paltz.

Colophon

The text was set in Palatino Linotype with headers in Casablanca Light SF with initials proportionally enlarged. The book was designed by the author in MS Word and then converted to PDF format for the printer using Adobe Acrobat.

The pre-Shang Dynasty pictograms throughout were hand-drawn on a Wacom Graphire 4 digital tablet by the author. Excepting the first, which comes from the title, they are the names of hexagrams from the *I Ching*, and they appear as follows:

Cover: *Yi (I)*—change, easy
Dedication, page v: *Shi*—chronicler
Page 18: *Ko (Ge)*—revolution, skinning, molting
Page 41: *K'un*—receptive, feminine, earth
Afterword, page 85: *Huà*—change, dissolve, pass away

The word *colophon* comes from the name of an ancient Greek city, one of the twelve Ionian cities that—according to Lucian's *True History*—might have been the birthplace of the epic poet Homer.

Other books by Heinz Insu Fenkl

Memories of My Ghost Brother
Bo-Leaf Books
www.boleafbooks.com

Kŏri: The Beacon Anthology of Korean American Fiction
(co-edited with Walter K. Lew)
Beacon Press
www. beacon.org

Century of the Tiger: 100 Years of Korean-American Immigration
(co-edited with Jenny Run Foster and Frank Stewart)
University of Hawai'i Press
www.uhpress.hawaii.edu

Forthcoming in 2007:
Korean Folktales: In the Old, Old Days
When Tigers Smoked Tobacco Pipes
Bo-Leaf Books
www.boleafbooks.com

For other writings, you may also visit Heinz Insu Fenkl's
webpage at: http://www.geocities.com/gnoth7